Believe in Yourself

... the Key to extraordinary
accomplishments and
personal fulfilment
in life.

Tim Oparaji

Published by New Generation Publishing in 2021

Copyright © Tim Oparaji 2021

First Edition

The author asserts the moral right under the Copyright, Designs and Patents Act 1988 to be identified as the author of this work.

All Rights reserved. No part of this publication may be reproduced, stored in a retrieval system or transmitted, in any form or by any means without the prior consent of the author, nor be otherwise circulated in any form of binding or cover other than that which it is published and without a similar condition being imposed on the subsequent purchaser.

Paperback ISBN: 978-1-80369-041-4
Hardback ISBN: 978-1-80369-042-1

www.newgeneration-publishing.com

New Generation Publishing

Contents

Dedication- To Pastor Chijioke Okonkwo	iv
Acknowledgment	v
Preface	viii
Introduction	x
Chapter One - The Power Of Self-Belief	1
Chapter Two - Discovering Your Real Self	17
Chapter Three - Rebuilding, Rebranding And Restoring Your Self-Esteem	33
Chapter Four - The Power Of Consistent Self-Improvement	59
Chapter Five - The Process Of Life Transformation	69
Chapter Six - Destiny Is Calling	87
Chapter Seven - If You Must Succeed, Believe In Yourself	105
Chapter Eight - The Power Of Mental Overhauling	133
Chapter Nine - If You Must Succeed, Believe In Your Ideas And Dream	145
Chapter Ten - Put Your Dream To The Test	169
Chapter Eleven - Africa, We Must Believe In Ourselves To Rise	185
Conclusion	206
About The Author	209

DEDICATION- TO PASTOR CHIJIOKE OKONKWO

This book is dedicated to Pastor Chijioke Okonkwo, who believes so much in me and sacrificed so much to invest in me as a demonstration of his belief in my potentials and capacity to achieve my dreams. His life has inspired and taught me to believe in myself and fight for the future I greatly desire. His personal life story is an inspiration to many people and stands as a proof that self-belief is the key to personal achievement and fulfilment in life.

Thank you for teaching me how to fight for my faith in my future. Thank your for pointing me to the great future even when I wasn't seeing it, your life is a compass to the young people who are seeking for direction in life and you have proven your faith in me and many other young people by your benevolence and philanthropic gesture towards our growth and development.

You are indeed an epitome of an uncommon mentor and father who believes in the future of his protege who have no hope of survival or success, a light that shines in the darkness of the poor and needy, thank you for putting smiles on my face and for giving me a lifetime opportunity upon which the inspiration for this book was drawn. Virtually all hope was lost and all dreams dead before you came into my life; but you brought back life to my dead dreams and gave me a cause to still hang in there and fight for the future I dream of everyday. You are much loved and treasured always.

To the glory of God, I wholeheartedly dedicate this book to you!

Thank you and I love you unimaginably.

Tim Oparaji

ACKNOWLEDGMENT

This work is indeed a product of a dedicated personal life of continuous and consistent learning, growth and development. It is also the collective contribution of many people such as friends, mentors and teachers whose lives, works, materials, and my personal encounter with them, have contributed to make me better and who I am, and I am highly indebted to every one of them.

I absolutely believe that no one is self-made or can be self-made, because we were all helped by some people at different stages and points of our lives, either at birth or through school; each one of us has been greatly affected by other people in one way or the other. It's absolutely true that we are the sum total of our thoughts, decisions, experiences, choices and learning over the years, as well as the contribution of other people, as we thrive to achieve our dreams and fulfil the destiny every one of us has been called to fulfil.

There is no outstanding accomplishment in any endeavour without a team or group of people, or support of one individual or the other, as only great things can be achieved with the collective contributions of some other people. Here are just a few people to whom I wish to give my appreciation and who, in one way or the other, have made this work a reality:

To Mr Olugbenga David O. Ogunbode, the Director of Cornerstone College Cambridge, for his mentorship, guidance and inspiration to write this book within a short frame of time. Each of my previous books took me over five years to write, but he inspired and pushed me to write this book in less than three months. Thank you for making me stretch myself beyond the limits I placed on myself. I am mostly grateful for the support throughout my pre-MBA studies at the Cornerstone College, you made what seemed difficult easy for me, and I thank God our paths crossed.

Meeting your family was a huge blessing to me and I am grateful to your wife, Mrs Alma Ogunbode for the great role she has played in my life during my studies at the College, ensuring I was comfortable, may God bless your home.

To Mrs Gladys Olufunmilola Oyedoyin, the head teacher of Cornerstone College, thank you for your counsel, love and support and all the encouragement you gave to me. Meeting you has been a great blessing, especially all the sessions you had with me, thank you for helping me balance my studies with my career pursuit.

To Mr Philip & Mrs Elaine Malkin, the CEO of Littleport Auction Rooms, I want to deeply thank you for the care, love and wisdom I received from you while serving under your guidance. I am grateful for the opportunity and privilege to learn from you, I will forever be grateful for the time I spent with you and your family.

To all the staff of Littleport Auction Rooms, I salute everyone of you, working and learning from you all has made me a better person and I will forever be grateful to God that our paths crossed. Thank you all for being being exceptional.

To Pastor Abayomi Mosaku ,the state pastor of Winner's Chapel Cambridge, and his entire family, for his fatherly role and spiritual counsel all through the period of my studies at Cornerstone College Cambridge, I am deeply grateful for your support and encouragement during the tough times of my stay at Cambridge, I want to say big thank you.

I want to appreciate my bosom friend, Juliette Bruno, her husband and entire family for her support all through my stay at Cambridge, you are kindhearted ,loving, exceptional and amazing and I am thankful for your words of encouragement and inspiration during the challenging times.

To my spiritual parents in the Lord, Apostle Johnson and Rev. Dr. Lizzy Suleiman; and Rev. Dr. Fidelis and Pastor Gladys Ayemoba. Thank you all for the love and support I have always enjoyed from you. I am grateful for having you in my life sir, meeting you has given me the greatest lift of my life.

To Apostle Arome Osayi, your teachings have been a great source of inspiration, especially on the subject of making your identity revealed through prayer. Thank you for your inspirational and impactful teachings which has transformed my life so much.

To Deacon Peter and Deaconess Gladys Aggrey; and Pastor Godson and Mrs Nonye Uche, your continuous support and belief in what I can become has always been an inspiration to me. Thank you for your love and support all the way.

To my good friend Jacintha Ozeh, you have been a special friend and has been there all the way, encouraging and supporting me, thank you for your input and contribution towards making this book a success.

To Victory Adaeze Osondu, my special friend and fiancee, thank you for believing in me and standing by me all through, your faith in me inspires me a lot to become my best. You are quite a huge source of inspiration to me and I am happy having you in my life.

Finally, to the supreme God and creator of mankind, to my Lord Jesus Christ who supplies me with all the grace, strength and inspiration to write, the giver and keeper of life and the one that has given me all the abilities and potentials. Thank you and I love you LORD.

PREFACE

Living to your full potentials and capabilities is the key to becoming the best that you can, but this can't be achieved without first having belief in yourself and accepting who you are. There is nothing as painful as knowing that you can be more than you are, but unable to attain your desires because you don't know how to. There are many people in life living far below the optimum capacity and what they are capable of doing, and that is the reason behind the poverty of billions of people in different parts of the world. We have more people leading an unhappy and unfulfilled life, and the worse part of it is they feel incapacitated and believe there is absolutely nothing they can do to change anything; hence, they decide to accept the wrong belief that their place is at the bottom. There is nothing that can't be changed or altered, and it doesn't really take so much to make a change in one's situation. A little change either in the thought pattern or in the way you do things is enough to cause a tremendous and unimaginable change in your life. Changing little things such as the way you think, talk or act can make a whole lot of difference in your life and career.

CONTROLLED BY WHAT YOU BELIEVE
The power of self-belief is so strong that it controls everything about your life and destiny, but sadly most people are ignorant of this foundational basic truth that shapes our lives. There are many philosophies and beliefs that people hold onto so tightly, not knowing that these are their major limitations in life, and that changing them could change the course and direction of their lives forever. So many things have wrongly conditioned you to think and behave in certain ways and have placed limitations on you; and, if you try to break out from your own limitations, you will have to begin a

total overhaul of your life, from examining what you believe about yourself to every aspect of your life.

YOU NEED SELF-BELIEF TO BE COMPETENT

Being competent in what you do is the key to being successful in your career and everything you do. Many people have asked whether you have to be competent in what you do before you can be self-confident, or do you have to be self-confident in order to become competent? I believe you have to be self-confident in order to become competent in what you do because, if people have to be competent first before believing in themselves and develop a strong confidence in themselves, then many people will remain far below average and operate below their capacity and capability. The crucial importance of having self-belief is that such positive mental outlook will reposition you to act in a way that is consistent with the kind of person you dream to become and the future you really desire to fulfil. Believing in yourself will inspire you to work assiduously to achieve your goals, which enhances, reinforces and consolidates your confidence and belief in yourself and what you are capable of achieving.

The power of self-belief is unlimited and can transform and transition you from failure to success, mediocrity to greatness, poverty to prosperity and from defeat to victory.

INTRODUCTION

I remember while growing up as a little child, I had lots of dreams and imaginations in my heart. I desired to be great and influential in life, but didn't know how that was going to happen as no one around me lived the kind of life I had always imagined. And so, I was caught up between self-doubts and frustrations because I didn't know if I was ever going to be what I have always dreamt of becoming. As I grew older, I realised I found it difficult to integrate and mingle with people and couldn't talk to people about how I could become what I desired to be. I couldn't ask anyone around me because no one knew what was going on within me. I was so misunderstood and misinterpreted, I felt I was in the dark as I couldn't find anyone around me who felt the way I did, or was the epitome of the future I desired. So, it was really difficult for me.

Countless number of times I was told I couldn't become what I had dreamt and imagined I would become. I was constantly forced to do what I didn't want to do; I was labelled stubborn and proud because I couldn't fit into the lifestyle lived by the people I was surrounded by. That probably made me withdraw from the public because I was tired of the constant misjudgement and misinterpretation of my motives and actions. That bred self-doubt and lack of confidence in myself, because virtually everything I did was condemned and criticised. I was not given liberty to exercise my will and follow my wishes and heart's desires.

Within me, I knew something was crying out for expression, but no one listened to me. I cried for attention, but there were none who would listen to me. I felt so unwanted and irrelevant before people; my opinion was never counted; I was seen by people, but was never heard nor given the benefit of the doubt. I was never allowed the

INTRODUCTION

freedom to be myself. I lived in fear, self-doubt, with feelings of worthlessness without any sense of healthy self-image and esteem. This trailed my life and I became somewhat violent, because I wanted to be heard and listened to. I was so scared of appearing in public, or even making my voice heard. Many people who didn't know me took it to mean I was a quiet boy, not knowing I was only withdrawn into myself as a means of protection from being criticised, condemned and rejected if I expressed myself.

Thanks to God, my aunty Khun, who took care of me after her mum, whom I lived with, passed on, decided to enrol me into the boarding school where I had fellow students to associate with. That became the first window of opportunity I had to express myself. The first book I ever read was given to me as a gift by the school, Wesley High School Otukpo, as the best graduating student in Mathematics/Physics. The book made a whole lot of difference in me and helped me to unleash my imaginative powers. The book was *The Magic of Thinking Big*, by David J. Shwartz. That was how I began to believe in myself once again, but it took several years because I had lost confidence in myself and because I wanted acceptance and approval from people. My joy and happiness were regulated by how people treated me, by public opinion, acceptance and approval; and I had to lead a double life because I wanted to fit into everyone's ideology and philosophy, as I thought I needed to please and be accepted by everyone in order not to be criticised, condemned or rejected.

The more I tried to please everyone to get their approval and acceptance, the more frustration and displeasure I felt. I always had to displease myself in order to make people happy so that they would accept me. Don't get me wrong, there's nothing wrong with displeasing yourself to help people, but doing it for the purpose of being accepted and approved by others is very wrong, because human beings are not the best kind of people to impress in life. I felt something wasn't right within me; I knew many things were wrong, but I didn't know what to do. I was so scared of rejection, criticism and condemnation such that, later in life, if I was genuinely rebuked or corrected by my superiors, I would automatically get angry and withdraw. I wanted everyone's approval, so any effort at correcting me was seen and perceived as rejection and condemnation. The worst of it was that there was no one whom I could confide in, whom I could pour out my grief to, whom I could learn from. My life was a personal struggle of trying to find my place in life and feel good about myself.

That book unlocked the passion to read and, as I continued reading books, especially inspirational and motivational books, I discovered that I needed to believe in myself to excel and fulfil my dreams. I realised self-belief was indispensable if I was ever going to achieve my dreams. As I began to look up to great authors whose books inspired me, one thing became so clear to me: I didn't need public approval or people's acceptance to believe in and feel good about myself. I realised it was my responsibility to rebuild, rebrand and restore my damaged self-image and chart another path for myself. Over the period of continuous and consistent transformation, many of those people around me are still surprised about how I have evolved to become who I really am today, especially the fact that I am writing books, because I was far from the person they see today.

Your destiny and future is trapped within you. No one has seen, or can ever imagine, what you are capable of becoming in life. You don't really know what you can be and are capable of accomplishing unless you believe in yourself; believing in yourself can transport your life from where you currently are to the realm of unimaginable success and greatness. I have realised that self-belief and confidence are the greatest key to personal victory, success and outstanding accomplishment in life; without those things, you will just accept the opinion that people have of you. If you don't believe in yourself, you will prove people right over what and who they say you are;

and, in most cases, it will always be a wrong and negative description of yourself, your capabilities and what you can achieve.

It doesn't matter if people have negative opinions of you or have told you that you are worthless. You don't really have to fight them; the secret is being able to believe in yourself enough, and you will be surprised to experience the power of self-belief and confidence.

I can't count the number of ladies whom I asked out that rejected me on the account of their inability to see a great future in me. Do you really know what it means to be humiliated and rejected by the ladies you admire as a young man? But, as time passed, I proved them all wrong; some even came back to me, but it was too late. If you will just believe in yourself to pursue your dreams, you will prove people wrong about their perception and description of who they thought you were.

EXPERIENCING THE LIMITLESS POWER OF SELF-BELIEF

You don't know the power of self-belief until you put it into practice. No one can write exhaustively on this subject because the best way to understand the power of self-belief and confidence is to believe in yourself and experience the unimaginable and unlimited possibilities that lie within you, because the human vessel or mind is an infinite elastic entity. You can't over stretch your human mind; there is no limit to the possibilities that lie within the human powers, so don't ever limit yourself to an ordinary life.

There is more; you deserve much more than what you are currently. It doesn't matter the level and heights you have attained; there is more. What you have accomplished is not all there is to achieve and accomplish in life. The world is plagued with so many problems and challenges; there was never a time when the world needed more saviours, solution providers and thinkers than the present time and the generation we are in. Many things are wrong and there are infinite things to be accomplished to make the world a safer and better place for us and the next generation; and only the power of self-belief can create a niche and give you a place in this world.

Don't be comfortable with leading an ordinary life without any influence and impact; change makers are in dire demand in our generation because of the challenges of the present times and what is yet to come upon us. Don't just sit down and watch things happen or wonder why things happen as they do; take up responsibility, be responsible for the success and betterment of the people and the world around you. Put yourself under pressure to serve your generation and improve the lives of people around you; make it your responsibility to see things improved and get better. Put the pressure and burden of your family's success and greatness on you. Take it up as a challenge to lift your family from poverty and mediocrity. Let your family and the people around you be happy because you were born in this time; rise up against a life of no influence and insignificance.

THERE'S MORE TO LIFE THAN WHERE YOU ARE
There is more to life than what and where you currently are. Only the power of self-belief will unleash the powers that reside within you. Make your voice heard. You can't read this book and relegate yourself to a life of penury and smallness. You can delve into an uncharted course, you can do what hasn't been done; you can accomplish anything you put your mind to. You will become an amazement to yourself and the people around you if you begin to believe in yourself, talk and take actions that are consistent with what you believe about yourself.

The secret is, let there be a fusion and harmony between your beliefs, values, talk and actions. Let your thoughts, about whom you believe yourself to be, match your words and actions. There's nothing in this world that can stop you.

INTRODUCTION

The problem with most people is, their words or actions are inconsistent with their heart, or what they think about themselves or believe about themselves. In the following pages of this book, you will discover great treasures and secrets that will equip you for a life of great accomplishment, greatness and fulfilment. Follow me as I guide you through this self-transforming journey into a life of limitless success, greatness and fulfilment.

'The only person who can pull me down is myself, and I'm not going to let myself pull me down anymore.'

— **C. JoyBell C.**

CHAPTER ONE
THE POWER OF SELF-BELIEF

'You may be the only person left who believes in you, but it's enough. It takes just *one star* to pierce a universe of darkness. Never give up.'
—Richelle E. Goodrich

I have often realised that many people believe in God, and in other people but themselves, and that is a critical factor behind their inability to lead a fulfilling life. It is easier for people to believe the words of other people, their thoughts and ideologies, but not themselves. I have observed that many people can easily accept what other people think about themselves, believe in other people's judgement and perception of themselves, and even go on to fulfil the expectations that other people have of themselves. But that is the reason behind their unhappy and unfilled life. The subject of self-belief can't be over emphasised because virtually everything you will ever achieve on Earth will be predicated on the subject of self-belief.

The subject of success and accomplishments in life is greatly connected to the power of self-belief, because no man can go beyond the level of his capacity to dream and imagine greatness. Great things are first conceived in the mind before they are translated into physical reality, and your ability to believe in your dreams and pursue them is the singular most critical factor in determining the extent of your greatness on Earth. A lot of people doubt their own ideas, their power to succeed and achieve great things in life because of a lack of self-belief, but a rich and rewarding life can't be separated from self-belief.

THE CONCEPT OF SELF-BELIEF?

Contrary to many people's opinion that self-belief is arrogance, pride and being rude, that is not true. Self-belief is an internal empowering and convincing feeling you have within you that there is nothing impossible. It is the momentum of life that gives one confidence and courage to stand up to, and overcome, any ugly circumstance of life that confronts you. It is that feeling of 'yes I can'. As a wise man says, 'If you believe you can, then you can, but if you don't believe you can, then you can't'. It is all about what you believe of yourself.

SELF-BELIEF IS THE FULCRUM OF DESTINY

Self-belief is the fulcrum of life. It is the centre of your life, the driver's seat of your destiny. That is where everything emanates from; that is where your life is given direction from; that is what gives direction to your life. Self-belief gives balance to life; it is the centre of balance in your life. It is so crucial and important to understand that self-belief is the common denominator of great men; they first believed in themselves before they were able to achieve great things – which, in turn, compelled the world to believe in them. If you don't believe in yourself, you will have no direction in life, because you will always be influenced by the opinions of other people, causing your life to be without direction, focus, power and energy.

SELF-BELIEF IS THE FOUNDATION OF PERSONAL SUCCESS

In my personal walk with great men and my study of their secrets of success and greatness, I have often observed that a great man leads a more private life, because they believe more in themselves than the world believes in them. That means that the foundation of personal success is self-belief and that, without it, there can never be personal achievement, success or greatness in life. When studying the secrets of great men, I have observed that 'they do their own thing'. They don't think much about 'what people think about them'; they are mostly concerned about what they think about themselves. The focus is more on themselves, their ideologies, philosophies, beliefs, perception of things, idiosyncrasies; it is first about whom they are. The foundation of personal success and greatness is self-belief, upon which other elements and factors of success and greatness like discipline, diligence, commitment and hard work are built.

Around this foundation, the fabric of greatness is weaved and the walls of success are erected. In other words, if you don't believe that you can succeed, or that you have all it takes to excel in life, you can never be committed to any goals or higher meaning of life. People naturally don't commit to any venture or pursuit they don't believe in. The pursuit of greatness and personal success emanates from the corner of self-belief.

SELF-BELIEF IS THE POWER PLANT OF GREAT ACCOMPLISHMENT

Self-belief is the power engine of great and successful men, because that is where their lives are powered to achieve their goals. Anyone who doesn't believe in the self can't go far or do much in life. In studying the attributes and factors behind the extraordinary achievement of people, I discovered that one major success denominator of successful men is the factor of self-belief. They usually believe in themselves beyond other people's doubts and wrong perception and judgement of them. Just like electricity powers your electrical appliances, in the same way self-belief powers your life for great accomplishments. It is the secret of great and successful men.

There is nothing like extraordinary men; there are only ordinary men who believe in themselves enough to do extraordinary things. The place of self-belief cannot be over emphasised in the journey of greatness and impact. It is the hallmark of all great men, because there will be a time in your life when nobody will believe in you, including the people you trust and expected to support you. Only the power of self-belief will keep you going. It is that internal fortitude and momentum that gives you the consciousness of self-reliance that makes you believe you can achieve anything, whether the world believes in you or not. This is the secret of great men, because there will always be times of loneliness and isolation when people fail to understand you because you have refused to subscribe to the status quo, which most people in the world are comfortable with.

When you make up your mind to do great things, some people will criticise you, some will withdraw from you and some will even oppose you; and, in the midst of this, the only power that will keep you standing strong and resilient is self-belief. Such moments must come in a man's life; it is the path of greatness and extraordinary accomplishment. If you continue to live an ordinary life, I can assure you that you will face no stiff opposition; but the moment you decide to make a change in your generation, then be ready for the heat because hell is going to be let loose on you. Every form of opposition will come your way, including from the people you love, your friends, your family members and even those you look up to, because people will always expect you to be small, to remain small, to play along with mediocre, to maintain the status quo and not to be greater than they are. It is normal in life. But don't be discouraged and disappointed, because that is the true and greatest test of your conviction of whom you truly are and your desire for change.

SELF-BELIEF SAVES YOU FROM NEGATIVE INFLUENCES AND PUBLIC OPINIONS

In my study of great men, I have discovered that it is natural for people to want to talk you down, especially when you are making progress in a direction that they didn't respect. People are going to rise up against you when you decide to do some great things beyond their imagination, especially

THE POWER OF SELF-BELIEF

when it has never been done by them. This is normal. Let's take President Donald Trump, former president of the United States, as an example. He was one president that faced criticism, both internally and internationally, during his four years in office. During his campaign, the media was against him, even some nations were against him, and virtually everybody was against him, but he didn't give in. He stood up to the challenge and achieved his dream of becoming the 45th President of the United State.

You need that measure of boldness and self-belief to be able to rise up in the face of cruel and vicious criticisms of haters and naysayers in order to achieve your dream. There will always be negative influences from people who don't want you to move ahead; you have to understand that not everyone will support you. There will be people who are going to rise up against you to stop you from fulfilling God's assignment and purpose for your life. 'People are always threatened by progress and change.'

You will always meet those who don't even know you but will speak against you; there are going to be those who will conspire to bring you down. You're going to meet a lot of people who will fight their way just to see you go down, because people are usually threatened by progress and change. If you always listen to what people have to say, or you are always concerned by what people say about you, then you cannot go far in life. I found that one key secret of great men is they don't think much about what people think about them; they are only concerned about what God thinks of them and what they think about themselves. People will always have an opinion about you and they are free to think about you in any way they like. People will always talk about you and they are free to talk about you any way they like – it is normal. I have also found that great men are not always looking for public approval or the approval of others. No! They are confident in themselves, and believe that they are able to achieve whatever they set out to achieve.

SELF-BELIEF UNLOCKS YOUR GENIUS

You may not have noticed this, but it is something I've observed in my personal life, that there were certain times in my life when I was alone and faced challenges. With no one to run to for help or assistance, suddenly in the moment of self-isolation I was able to come up with ideas and solutions to the challenges I was facing. So, I discovered that self-reliance, conviction and self-belief will always unlock your genius (for further reference within the context of this writing, I use 'self-reliance' to mean looking up to God who dwells in you, because the Greater One lives in you as believer in Christ Jesus and I uphold the belief that man is insufficient on his own without God and the help of God which come through the channels of men he sends to us).

The major problem with the third world – namely, Africa – is that it is constantly and consistently dependent on the industrialised nations of the world for everything, even toothpicks, and this factor has blocked and locked up its potentials and geniuses. The moment you decide to cut yourself off from external sources, help and assistance, and look inward into yourself, you will always unlock the sleeping giant within you. You will always discover that there is a sleeping giant within you, but it has been locked up because you never paid attention to it. You might have been busy looking externally for help, but the moment it becomes your nature to always depend on and look up to people for everything, you will never be creative; you will never be self-reliant and self-dependent, and that will lock your abilities and capacity for greatness. Great people always look inwards and depend on themselves to come up with solutions to their problems; this is one of the powers and benefits of self-belief.

Take a moment to reflect on your own life. There may have been times when you found yourself in a precarious situation where reaching out to people for help was difficult or impossible. In that moment of self-dependence and reliance, you came up with solutions and ideas that saved you from that. Everyone is born with divine intelligence, wisdom, gifts and talent to help them navigate life, and help them through challenges and limitations. The best way to give expression to these innate abilities is to be self-reliant and self-dependent, and to believe in yourself that you have all it takes to excel and make the most of life. Just like every seed has in itself the fruits, tree, leaves, branches and stem, and that all it needs to release its powers is to be planted in the right environment; just as everything is already within the seed, so it is with us. All the things we need to maximise our lives were inbuilt at birth, and it will require self-development and engagement of our minds to release our potentials.

When a child is born, for example, who teaches the baby where his mouth is, or where the mother's breast nipples are, or how to put the nipple into his mouth? Why didn't he put it in his nose or another place? This is because we are all born with natural gifts and abilities to help us navigate life and find solutions to the problems in our lives. However, you might never discover your greatness until you become self-reliant, dependent and believe in your capacity to excel.

SELF-BELIEF OPENS YOU UP TO OPPORTUNITIES AND MULTIPLIES YOUR POSSIBILITIES
(Philippians 4:13)

If a man believes in himself and in his ability and capacity to find the answers and solutions to the problems and questions of his life, he will always be drawn to places of opportunities, and his ability to maximise opportunities and do great things will be multiplied. That is to imply that, when you believe that you can, you will always find the ways. As the popular adage goes, 'If there is a will, there will always be a way'. It is a divine default system God built within man to help man navigate life and its challenges; the system was built inside of us to always point us to places of opportunities and to make us see possibilities in the midst of challenging opposition and limitations.

For example, let's take the case of a newborn baby that

automatically knows where his mother's nipples are and how to direct it into his mouth. It's when you begin to believe in the greatness that resides within you that your perspective changes from seeing oppositions to opportunities; consequently, your possibilities will be multiplied, meaning you'll be able to see possibilities in the midst of those opportunities that seem to be obstacles, limitations and challenges for others. You will suddenly see yourself doing great and unimaginable things. When you hear stories of men who are doing things that nobody has ever done, it is because they saw possibilities in the opportunities which others saw as obstacles and challenges.

What believing in yourself does to you is that it helps you to ask 'How can I do this?' 'What is the way forward?' 'How do I do it?' Others, however, will always ask, 'Is this possible?' Those that see challenges and obstacles will always ask, 'Is this possible?' 'Can this ever be done?' But those that see opportunities will always ask the right questions that unlock the genius that is within, such as 'How can I do this?' 'How do I find the solution?'

Once you ask the right questions, the right answers will become accessible. Statements such as 'God, please show me the way forward', 'I believe I can do this', 'I believe I can handle this', 'I believe I can find the solution', 'I believe I can find the answer', will unlock your creativity and the sleeping giant and, sooner than later, you will find yourself in a world of limitless possibilities and people will think you are an extraordinary superman. However, that is not necessarily the case; it's just that you are able to believe in yourself enough to tell yourself that you can, which unlocks your genius and leads you into the world of limitless possibilities.

That is why the Holy Bible says,

I can do all things through Christ (who dwells in me) and strengthens me.

Philippians 4:13

SELF-BELIEF EMPOWERS YOU TO BE ORIGINAL – BEING YOURSELF

Whenever you see a sign of inferiority complex in a man, it points to the fact that such a person lacks confidence and self-belief. An inferiority complex is one of the greatest signs that a person doesn't believe in himself or in his own ability to succeed. Whenever you see someone who doubts himself, his ideas, identity, or loses faith and confidence in himself, his tribe or nation, and in what he can do, it shows you that such a person doesn't believe in himself, and that is the worst thing that can happen to a person.

I regret to say this and I mean no harm to anyone, but it is rather misleading to have many mentors and role models emphasise the idea of followership, stressing the inevitable place of younger ones learning from them and following their footsteps and principles to excel in life, without also emphasising that they should not lose their own identity in the course of following them. What many mentors and fathers see as genuine followership is if their mentees or followers dress the same way as they do, talk the same way, and do the same things as them, while forgetting the truth that God didn't create two persons alike.

As such, something that fits you or works for you might not work for the other, because our ASSIGNMENTS AND PURPOSES are different. God didn't create two persons to do the same thing at the same time. Jesus Christ made this clear by giving five different folds of ministry and different kinds of gifts and patterns of operations (Ephesians 5:11, 1 Corinthians 12:4-12). Many people have over-exaggerated the idea of 'imitating people' to be successful; but imitating someone doesn't mean you should lose your identity, originality and nature.

'You can only be you, and it is only you that can be you.'

No matter how well you try to copy another person or to become like another person, you will end up deformed from your originality because you can never become exactly like another person. You can only be yourself, you can only be you, and it is only you that can be you. God didn't create you to act like another person. He didn't create you to transform yourself into another thing He didn't originally create you to be, He created you to be whom He wants you to be. So, when you see a person trying to change himself or herself to become another person he wasn't designed to be at birth – changing their originality as designed by God – that is the highest manifestation of inferiority complex and lack of self-confidence and belief in one's capabilities and capacity. Sure, we do learn from others, but we are not to lose ourselves and identities. Learn from others to be successful, but don't eventually lose yourself. Maintain your originality and naturally, that is where your uniqueness lies.

Following the footsteps of fathers and mentors doesn't mean you should lose your originality, it doesn't mean you should be lost in them; rather, you should find yourself, your purpose, path and pattern. You must not lose your identity because your identity is what defines your life and destiny; it is what makes you different from another person because, in this world, no two persons have the same fingerprints. God didn't make any two persons the same. If the over 7 billion people on the face of the Earth have different fingerprints, it means that everybody is different and everybody has a distinct contribution to make to their generation. You don't have to copy what another person is doing in order to become successful, but you can learn how they think and follow their footsteps, principles, philosophies and sometimes their ways or pattern (but which might not fit your makeup) in order to discover your own self and identity.

LIVING YOUR OWN LIFE

Whenever you see a successful man, you will often observe that they exude great poise and drive, power and motivation, confidence and courage and, more often than not, you will

> *The great obstacles of life lie within and not without.*

probably think that they are super beings from another planet. They are people who exhibit the 'I can' attitude and this is the attitude that sets other qualities and attributes in motion. Without self-belief, nothing else works. Taking a look at my own life, I realised that, most often at the root of failure and defeats, lack of self-belief is usually traceable. For instance, in retrospect, think about when your teacher asked a question and you knew the answer but was afraid to raise your hand to answer, until someone else stood up and answered the question.

Think about other times when you knew the answer or solution to a particular question or problem, either at your place of work, school or other public events, but you couldn't stand up and step forward to speak up, and how you felt when someone else spoke up and probably won the prize. Think about how you felt within yourself for not standing up to speak up. Think about how if affected your mood, self-image and personality! Well, I wasn't an exception. It happened to me many times, more than it happened to you, so don't feel bad.

Self-debilitating thoughts, lack of self-belief and trust in one's life are probably the greatest obstacles you will have to overcome in order to achieve your goals in life. Internal obstacles and limitations are worse than external obstacles, and the greatest enemy you will probably have to deal with for the greater part of your life is your 'self'. Dealing with a limiting and defeating mindset will be the greatest challenge of your life in the journey of greatness and self-actualisation.

> *A man who can't conquer himself can't conquer his world*

LIFE IS LIVED INSIDE-OUT

The great obstacles of life lie within and not without. A man who can't conquer himself can't conquer his world, because

Believe in Yourself

life is lived inside-out. Life is lived from within. The external circumstances of your life are a reflection of your internal world. We lead life from within. Don't be so carried away with what is happening in the outside world of your life that you neglect to pay greater attention to your internal world. If you must lead a great life, then you must pay attention to what happens within – not without.

> *You can change the outcome of your life by changing the thoughts of your mind*

Someone said to me that his job was unsatisfying and he was merely getting by with it, that the job is draining life out of him. I immediately responded, 'Then change it, leave the job and get a better one.' He responded, 'No!' He said that he couldn't do anything about it because, in a foreign country that is not yours, you can't choose what kind of job you do. That the menial jobs are for the blacks! And I said, 'That is where your problem is – your mind.' Your thinking!

You see, you can change the outcome of your life by changing the thoughts of your mind because your thoughts shape your perception, your perception produces your words and your worlds produce your actions, which produce your character. And that leads to your attitude that ultimately interprets and gives explanation to your external world – the circumstances of your life. When you believe you can't change anything, then you won't be able to change it. Everything depends on your perception and the interpretation you give to them. There is nothing that can't be changed in life.

> *Matthew 12:37 a good man out of the good treasures of his heart brings forth good things and an evil man out of the evil treasure of the heart brings forth evil things.*

TWO WORLDS

Every man has two worlds – the internal world and the external world. The internal world has to do with what goes

THE POWER OF SELF-BELIEF

on within yourself. That is where the true life is led. You are first rich in the inner world before you can become rich in the outer world. You first become great, successful, victorious, powerful, unbeatable AND prosperous in this internal world, before you can become the same outside.

Prosperity is an offspring of the inner life, success and greatness is an offspring of the inner life, and a rich and fulfilling life is also an offspring of this inner life. In this vein, an unproductive life, a defeated life, an unhappy and unfulfilled life is also an offspring of the inner life. Whatever a woman is pregnant with, is what she will deliver.

> *It is Your inner life that gives birth to your outer world*

When a woman gives birth to a child, whether male or female, it is a product she conceives in the womb – the inner world. So, the inner world gives birth to the outer world. You don't change the outer world by trying to change the circumstances of the external world; don't spend too much of your time trying to affect those external circumstances of your life – that is not where life happens. The external world is the show room, the display room of the workshop – the internal world. The internal world is the workshop where the goods and products of your life are first conceived, designed, fabricated and eventually reproduced or manufactured and then taken into the external world for display for all to see.

The defects in products are not corrected in the market place! When the producers display their products in the public and people get to buy them, if there is a complaint from the buyers and users of the products, the producers do what we call 'product recall' and the essence is to take it back to their production room and correct the defects. They don't correct the defects in the market place. So, if you discover your products in life, your outputs, your external circumstances are not good, full of unsatisfaction, unhappiness, failures, worries, defeats, and unfulfilling, then call back yourself into your centre of production, the room where you designed

Believe in Yourself

and manufactured it. Check your heart, your mind, for that is where the problem is.

Proverbs 23:7. For as a man thinks, so is he. When you understand this protocol of life fulfilment and progress, you won't waste your energy in the wrong place. Knowing the right place to invest your resources and energy is as important as having great ideas and strategies.

If you don't believe in yourself, no one will ever believe in you

The reason many people are not happy or making progress in life is because they spend their efforts and resources in the wrong place and consequently get worn out.

Your success in life depends much more on you than it depends on others

The internal world can also be referred to as the imaginative world, where civilisation takes place. For instance, everything you see in the external world today was an idea in someone's internal or imaginative world. The computers we use, the cars we drive, the aeroplanes we fly, the clothes we wear, the books we read – everything that you see in the external world first existed in someone's internal or imaginative world. Your great responsibility will be how to relate and manage your internal world, because that is where life is truly led from.

You must believe in yourself if you want to succeed in life because, if you don't believe in yourself, it is most likely that no one will believe in you. Your success in life depends much more on you than it depends on others. It doesn't matter what people think about you, the question is what are you thinking about yourself? What do you think about yourself? Who do you see yourself becoming in life? What do you think you can achieve in life? What do you believe you can do? What do you believe you were born to do? What is your perception about your life? Who do you believe you are?

'Don't get confused between what people say you are and who you know you are.'

—Oprah

CHAPTER TWO
DISCOVERING YOUR REAL SELF

'Know thyself.' —Socrates

The primary and major reason that makes people doubt themselves and lose faith and confidence in themselves, resulting in a feeling of inferiority complex and insignificance, is ignorance of whom they are, their real selves and identity. When a man knows who he really is, he will never feel inferior, neither will anyone look down on him because no one can make you feel inferior without your permission. The subject of knowing who you really are is the foundation or launchpad for great achievements, as no one can actually succeed beyond the level he is able to believe in himself and in his capacity to excel in life. The day you discover yourself is the day you discover your significance in the world. As you probably know, there are two important days in every man's life: the day a man is born and the day he discovers his purpose and significance for living.

I have observed in the lives of people – and, of course, in my own personal life, when I was much younger than I am now – that lack of self-knowledge, self-awareness or ignorance of who you really are is the major reason why people don't attempt or achieve great things in life. It's the reason why people ignore you and treat you with disdain and disrespect. I have seen a lot of people who don't have much money, or material possessions as such, but are highly respected and treated with honour and dignity even beyond those that have many material things. That goes to say that it is not just money or material possessions that attract dignity and respect from people, but the quality of life you lead as a result of your personal discovery of who you are.

When you discover who you are, you naturally feel like

a superman; you feel great about yourself, you have a sense of significance and joy about yourself and that affects your whole life, your attitude, the way you talk and the way you do things. People will naturally see you exude an attitude of power, courage and confidence even when you don't have much money. Knowledge of yourself naturally makes you lead a life of integrity, which is the bedrock of lasting success and greatness. The knowledge of self-significance changes everything about you. You start talking like a success, you talk big things, dress appropriately to look like you know where you are going; you dress like the address of your future, and talk like the future you see, and eventually start walking your talk, which is the path of self-transformation that leads to greatness.

There is no man that discovers his true self and significance in the world and ever leads an intimidated, fearful and ordinary life or subscribes to a lesser life than he deserves. Such a person will rise up from the crumbs of life and reach the stars in the sky; he will rise up from the valley of slavery and reach the palace of kingship; he will rise up from the ranks of the poor and thrive to reach the ranks of the rich. That is what knowledge of your real self will do to you.

REDISCOVERING A MISPLACED IDENTITY

There is story once told by Dr. Myles Monroe about a lion cub that lost his identity among sheep, and then lived a false image of himself as a sheep and behaved as a sheep until the very day the stark reality of who he really was dawned on him. It was a lion cub that was separated from his family in the forest and was suddenly found by a farmer, who took his herd of sheep into the forest for grazing. He then decided to take the lion cub home and raised him among the sheep for several years. One day, the farmer took the herd of sheep and the lion for grazing and eventually went to a river to drink water. While they were all drinking from the river, a big lion came out from the forest and roared across the river and they all fled for safety into their farm house.

One fateful day while they all grazed, the young lion went into the river alone to drink water, and when the lion dipped his face he saw an image of the lion they had ran away from previously. He thought that the same lion had come after them, so he jumped out of the river and ran backwards, but none of the other sheep ran with him. On the one hand, he was surprised that the sheep didn't run while, on the other hand, the sheep were also stunned as they saw the lion fleeing backwards. It caused confusion among them. Then, after a short while the big lion came out again and roared and the sheep fled for their lives. However, before the lion could step out of the water, the big lion was already in the water and growled at him, staring at him in the face. In desperation, the small lion tried to roar back to the bigger lion, but couldn't produce the same sound, for he sounded like a sheep. After several attempts, he was able to roar exactly like the big lion. Then he realised he was like him and that was how he discovered his identity as a lion. He went with the big lion into the forest to lead the true life he was originally designed to live.

Many people lead a life of fear, timidity, poverty, mediocrity and intimidation because they haven't discovered their true selves, and that is why they have been living a false image of another life. If the reality of who you truly are dawns on you, you will not be where you are today; you will reach up for the stars in the sky, you will reach out for the best in life, and you will rise from the dunghill and dust of poverty and rise onto the plane of greatness and personal fulfilment.

The problem is not about people who treat you as insignificant or make you feel inferior; it is because of the wrong identity and false image you have presented to them.

People will always treat you from their perception of you, and that

'Until you discover who you truly are people will always tag you what you are not.'

Believe in Yourself

perception is furnished from the perspective of yourself that you present to them; and, most often, their perception of you will always be wrong, which is why they don't treat you with dignity and respect. The primary thing I want you to get out of this book is the necessity of knowing who you really are, because that is the most singular critical factor that will shape the rest of your life.

> *'The day a man discovers himself, a champion is born'*

My pain is, many people know a lot of people, I hear people take pride in the fact that they know a lot of successful and influential people in big positions in society and that hasn't changed their status. They know so many people, but don't know the most important person in the world, which is 'themselves'. **You are the most important person you need to know in this world** because **the day you know yourself, the world would desire to know you and to be associated with you**. This is why I want you to understand how critical knowing yourself is to achieving and fulfilling your dream. The world doesn't know you yet because you have not known yourself. In the next few pages, I will be sharing with you how to discover or know who you really are. That is the most crucial knowledge you need in this world to fulfil the destiny you have always dreamt of and lead an accomplished, rewarding and fulfilling life.

> *You are the most important person you need to know in this world*

THE PATH OF SELF-DISCOVERY

Many writers have written books on the subject of self-discovery and, sincerely, most of them are helpful because I've read many self-help books on the subject of discovering yourself and your purpose. This subject is very crucial because I believe the most important discovery on Earth is the discovery of yourself. Life truly begins with the discovery of your purpose on Earth. The day you discover yourself a giant is born! If you discover what you were born to be or the problem you were created to solve; life will become meaningful. Leading a fulfilled life is not completely feasible on Earth until you have discovered that specific assignment you were born to do, and that is the greatest responsibility of everyone on Earth.

I spent many years trying to discover who I really am, trying to find significance and purpose of my living and existence on Earth. I now want to share my insight with you from another perspective of my discovery on this subject, which is probably very different from the nuggets and insights you may find in most of the self-help books that have been written before. Even in my second book *Against All Odds,* I wrote about the subject of self-discovery, but as we grow in age and keep developing and growing, we also grow in knowledge and discovery. So, this is an addition to the knowledge of what I shared in that book on this subject of self-discovery.

THE MANUFACTURER AND THE PRODUCT

I would like to begin by using the concept of the 'designer of a product' and 'the product' itself. I was tempted to use the concept of the 'manufacturer' or the 'producer' and the products, but upon reflection I realise that a manufacturer or producer of a product might not necessarily be the designer of that product. For instance, I am the writer of this book but I did not produce or print the book, someone else did. I paid someone else who has the abilities and the technology or facilities to print books for me. There are many people who design products, but others may have manufactured or produced it. Another good example has to do with an architect and the builder; an architect might design a building and a builder will construct it, but the designer has more knowledge of the functionality of the product than even the manufacturer. So it goes well to state that the designer of a product has the best knowledge of the product than anyone else and, in order to know the real and accurate function of a product, one should consult the designer.

In chemistry, we were taught that, in order to study the behaviour and characteristics of a compound, you have to study the behaviour and characteristics of the individual elements that make up the compound, because the compound will always possess or exhibit at least some of the characteristics of its component elements. Therefore, I would like to describe the relationship between God the creator of all things including Man as the 'Designer' and also the 'Manufacturer', and the creation, including Man as the 'Products'.

The Creator created every other thing except Man after their own kind; meaning, that everything God created except Man is of their kind. For example, in order to study a goat to know its characteristics, you need to study a goat not a sheep or dog. If you want to study the behaviour of the lion, don't go to study the tiger simply because they are both wild animals or carnivores; you must study the lion because the lion wasn't created from another animal, there was no mutation or evolution from another animal. Also, if you want to study a mango fruit or tree, don't go to study an orange tree or fruit; if you need to study about a pineapple, don't go to an apple tree or fruit because they are of their own kinds. They didn't evolve from another parent fruit or tree; they are their own kinds and original. None of them was made from another kind!

Genesis 1:24-25, And God said, let the earth bring forth the living creature after his kind, ...And God made the beast of the earth after his kind, and cattle after their kind, and everything that creepeth upon the earth after his kind.

But when God wanted to make man, he didn't make man an original of himself, which therefore implies that man is a derivative of something else which is God Himself. When the creator wanted to make man, He made man from the

Godhead. He used his own self to make man because He said to the community of the Godhead, let us make man in our own image and after our likeness.

What does that mean? It means that man is an image and likeness of another being or personality which is God; man emanated or evolved from God and not monkeys or apes. That is to say, man is a photocopy of God, man was created to resemble and look like God and not

> *Genesis 1:26-27, And God said, let us make man in our image, after our likeness.... So God created man in his Own image, in the image of God created he him...*

himself. So, God is the reference of man; we were created to function like God and operate like Him, since we were made partly from the component of God. It therefore means that we are supposed to have the characteristics God, that we ought to behave like Him as His children, like they commonly say, 'like father like son'.

This is so because God is in the Trinity, meaning He manifests or dwells in three forms: the Father, the Son and the Holy Spirit. In like manner, He made man to be in three forms: the spirit, the soul and the body. In order for you to truly understand your true or real self, it is important to draw your reference from God. You have to go back to God, we must return to our maker and creator. You don't truly know yourself and what you are capable of doing until you discover what God says about you, and just as every designer of a product has a manual as a reference, so the Creator has a manual for His Product – Man – and that is His word (the Holy Bible).

The day you discover personally what God says about you in His word, your life will take a different meaning; it will change everything about you, your perception and mentality. It will completely alter and revolutionise your life and put you on a different pedestal of success, greatness, significance and fulfilment. Ever since I came in contact with His word about me, my life changed forever.

I remember the story of my Leadership mentor, Dr. Myles Munroe. He said that, when he was a teenager in secondary school, his teacher told him he would not amount to anything significant in life because he made poor grades in school. One day, he was studying the Word of God and stumbled on where God says, 'Now unto him that is able to do exceeding abundantly above all that we ask or think, according to the power that worketh in us. **Ephesians 3:20** He then said to himself, 'So the power to be great and do mighty things is already in me as a Christian, I have the power right within me, no man will deceive me again or call me a nonentity. I won't allow my teacher to dictate and determine the outcome of my life anymore.' That was how that discovery of his identity from the Designer's manual changed the course of his life forever. He went on to author bestselling books, his books being translated in over 30 different languages of the world. He received the OBE from the Queen of England, Queen Elizabeth II, he owned a private jet and lived a fulfilled life before his death.

However, it is important to know that there is a very high possibility of using a product outside its originally designed intent and purpose. For instance, an architect may design and build a house for residential purposes and eventually a new buyer or owner may turn it into a commercial or industrial use. Many times you will find some people are using a particular product for something it wasn't meant or intended for and that is an abuse. As Myles Munroe clearly states, 'When the purpose of a thing is not known abuse is inevitable.' Many people have been misusing so many products, and abusing them; most sadly is the fact that many people are not just abusing some products, but themselves.

Just as there is child abuse, using a child to do something that it is not supposed to do. In many nations of the world, there are laws prohibiting child abuse.

But most sadly, many people don't know they are self-abusing themselves by engaging in enterprises or assignments that the Creator didn't intend for them to do. When you engage in something that God didn't intend for you to do, it is an abuse of yourself; you are abusing your potential and capability. It does not matter how long you have travelled on a wrong road; you can never get to the right destination because right steps only lead to right results; the right direction leads to the right destination and it's never too late to turn from a wrong path

> *It does not matter how long you have travelled on a wrong road; you can never get to the right destination*

or course. It is time to get yourself acquainted with God to find out the purpose for which he created you.

YOUR WORK VERSUS YOUR JOB

On this subject of discovering yourself or your true identity, and your purpose on Earth, I would like to distinguish between two concepts that have been misused by so many people, and that is the concept of work and your job. Unfortunately, many people assume that their work is the same thing as their job and they spend all their lives on a job, earning salaries and paying bills. Many people assume that their job is what defines their lives, but that is not usually the case. What truly is your job, and what is your work? If you can understand these two concepts and distinguish between them, then you will be able to maximise your life.

To begin with, your job is simply what you are paid to do, while your work is what you were designed and born to do. Your job is endurable, while your work is enjoyable. Your job is what you only thank God for because 'It's Friday' and sad because 'It's Monday', while your work is what you thank God for every day. Your job is what you do stressfully and strenuously; but your work is what you do seamlessly. While most jobs exploit you, your work transforms you. You can be sacked or fired at your job, but you can never be sacked or fired at your work. Your job is where you go to every morning; your work is what you live for all the days of your life. Your job has no security, but your work is your security; your job comes from the external environment, but your work is internal, it comes from within. Your job can be threatened by your employer, but your work can never be threatened because your potentials, gifts and talents are your employer. You will retire from your job, but you cannot retire from your work; you outlive your job, but your work outlives you, it transcends generations. The world will always forget your job, but the world will always remember your work; your job can wear you out, but your work always empower you from within. Your job is what you change from one better paid job to another, but in your work you go from one level of growth and glory to another. You use your self-acquired skills primarily to do your job, but your work demands the use of your gifts, talents and your potentials. You may not be happy at your job, but you are always happy with your work; your job keeps you limited and confined, but your work continuously opens you up to more opportunities. Your job may make you successful in terms of material wealth acquisition, but only your work can make you successful and fulfilled in life. Your job is pay driven, but your work is impact driven and can make a difference.

Am I in any way against jobs? No! Your goal should be to get a good job, and a good job is one that helps you develop your gifts, talents and potential and prepares you for your life assignment or work. Any job that takes your peace, makes you happy only because it is Friday, that is full of stress and strain should not be considered; that is not adding to your life because it is supposed prepare and equip you for your lifetime assignment.

There are many instances where you may have a good job and also begin your work alongside; that is, you may not always have to quit your job to begin your work. For instance, you may be working for an organisation and still be running an NGO to take care of the less privileged; you may have your paid job and still be running a farm, hospital or be engaged in

DISCOVERING YOUR REAL SELF

reaching out to lives. That thing you do primarily to add value to the environment and lives around you is your work and I advise you to take up a job you naturally have flair for.

YOUR PURPOSE IS IN YOUR PASSION

Another principle of self-discovery is to discover where your passion lies, your drive. Your purpose will always be found in your passion, because every product was designed with the features to perform its function, meaning it's your purpose that determines your design. A manufacturer first thinks of what he wants to achieve, the reason or purpose of a thing, the gap he wants to fill, the needs he wants to meet before thinking of the kind of product design that can perform such a function.

'Purpose precedes design.'

So, having discerned what purpose or function the product is going to perform, the manufacturer goes to the drawing board to design the kind of product that will fulfil the purpose; that is why I said purpose precedes product design. Most of the time, your passion gives explanation to your design; it gives you insight and light for the reason why you were created just exactly the way you are.

Passion always points to your purpose.

Every product has an inbuilt feature to fulfil the purpose for which it was designed to do. So, you always have to ask yourself, what are you passionate about, what do you have flair for?

What can you do naturally? What are you willing to do if money was not a consideration? What are you willing to do for free? What are you willing to do even if no one is willing to pay you? What makes you feel pain the most? What makes you cry the most? What do you like discussing the most? Where does your interest lie? What is that thing that you cannot get off your mind?

PASSION COMES WITH INTEREST AND LIKES

It is important to understand that your passion or drive comes with some particular areas of interests; it streamlines your attention, interests and likes. You have to pay attention to the things you like, are attracted to all the time, the areas you like to visit, the kind of people you attract into your life. As little as these things may seem, they mostly help you to discern your purpose in life. It is good to pay attention to the things you naturally have tendencies and inclinations for, and that is where good parenting comes in.

Parents should be able to pay attention to their children when they are little because, at this period where they are free and have no inhibitions or capacity to think about choice of careers, to know about the injustices in the world, to know what the choices and alternatives are, they usually display their natural instincts and interests at this period, pointing to the direction of their purpose. Good parents should be discerning enough to know this and guide their children in the right direction.

If you were to live in an ideal world where everything happens as it should be, where you don't have to do something else because you don't have an alternative or an option, what would you choose to do? That is where your purpose is. There are many people who do what they don't like to do simply because they don't have an option or alternative; if they had an alternative, they wouldn't be doing what they're doing now. It means they are not in the right place and therefore would never be fulfilled. Life is all about being fulfilled in what you do, everything else is secondary. You can always create what you want to do even if it's not in existence, that is where your purpose comes into play.

FOLLOW YOUR HEART AND INWARD LEADING

Like I said earlier, life is lived from within and one of the benefits of believing in yourself is that it will make you become your real self and live your own life instead of someone else's life. Sadly enough, we live in a world where most people are confused and have a misplaced identity and therefore live other people's lives, other people's choices and other people's decisions. However, the beauty of life is living your own life because life is lived from within, which means you will have to take responsibility for all of your actions and decisions; and, as a result, you must be willing to follow your heart.

There is a spirit within man, and a conscience in man, that always gravitates towards the direction that God has destined each individual to be, and it is paramount that you listen to your spirit always. This is especially if the other methods or paths to follow to discover yourself, as I explained above, may not specifically be consistent with your design and personality.

I know there are people who just lead a quiet life and their hearts, spirits or their conscience are their main guide given to them by God to direct them in the path of life and destiny. So, if you are such a person it will be very important that you always listen to your heart, listen to your spirit, and listen to what God is saying to you on your inside, because life is all about what is happening within you. Your external world is just a reflection of your internal world, hence you will have to pay attention to what goes on within you.

Every great man knows how to listen to himself, to that inner voice that is always craving for expression. Don't be lost in the crowd, moved by people's opinion because of the misconception that the highest number or vote is always right, for that is not always true. It is very possible that, in a class of a hundred students, a student can be right as against the 99 other students. For the singular reason that a particular opinion carries the highest number of votes or consents, it doesn't always make it right, that is why you have to live your own life and live by your own convictions.

Great men lead by their own convictions, not by the public's consensus.

Believe in Yourself

> *'It is too expensive to live other people's lives.'*

That is why you have to decide within you, what do I really want for myself? What do I want for my life? What makes me happy? What is my heart saying? What are my beliefs, values and convictions? What fits me? What is my purpose for being on Earth and why am I here?

These questions are peculiar to you and that is why you must always learn to listen to your heart, spirit and that inner voice that is always speaking to you on your inside, because more often than not they will always lead you to the right path and destination. I am saying this because, from my own personal experience and interviews with successful men, I realised that most of the decisions that I have taken in my life that resulted into failures and deep regrets were the decisions that were taken because of other people's opinions and influences, which I accepted responsibility for. And the biggest regrets I had were from those decisions that my heart was telling me otherwise. My spirit was grieved and my convictions were contradicted.

Somehow, within me I knew that this decision I was taking wasn't really okay and I didn't feel the inner peace, but I didn't have enough self-confidence and belief to say no to the public opinions and influences, and instead choose what was consistent with my convictions and aspirations. I was more concerned about my external environment, public opinion and pleasing everyone than listening to my heart, rather than following my convictions and acting in a manner that epitomised my values, beliefs and convictions.

I have learnt by experience that following my personal convictions will always save me from regrets. In my own opinion, I think it's better for one to regret the decisions he or she took by himself or herself than to regret the decisions taken because of people's influences and public opinions, of which their convictions and hearts were against.

Always listen to yourself, talk to yourself, and I assure

you, in the most critical situation or circumstance of life, and in the midst of millions of voices with dissenting opinions and perspectives, your heart and your spirit will always be there to speak to you and lead you in the right direction, but only if you are willing to listen to it and follow. But if you don't train and discipline yourself to always obey that voice within you, you will never maximise the benefits and values that it has to offer you.

'Believe in your infinite potential. Your only limitations are those you set upon yourself. Believe in yourself, your abilities and your own potential. Never let self-doubt hold you captive. You are worthy of all that you dream of and hope for.'

— Roy T. Bennett, The Light in the Heart

CHAPTER THREE
REBUILDING, REBRANDING AND RESTORING YOUR SELF-ESTEEM

'If you truly want to be respected by people you love, you must prove to them that you can survive without them.'
—Michael Bassey Johnson

I find it personally fulfilling and rewarding writing this book and most especially this particular topic, because I was a victim of an inferiority complex, lack of self-belief and lack of self-confidence in my childhood and teenage years. The reason for that was because I spent the greater number of my years living and serving people and, as a result, I was abused and molested in various ways. I was abused in some of the families or homes I had grown up in, the schools I had attended, the jobs I had taken, by some people I had served and by people who were bigger and higher than me. Yet, I know that there are millions of people in the world today who didn't have the privilege and opportunity of parental care and love as me.

Many people have had to go through different circumstances and situations in life just to get by and make ends meet, and in the process have been abused, their self-image damaged, their self-esteem destroyed, and their concept of themselves maligned, and this has greatly affected the person they have become in adulthood. I quite understand that most people today who feel bad about themselves, hate themselves and who lack self-confidence, were victims of one form of abuse or the other in the process of growing up, especially under the care of foster or surrogate parents.

Only a few such circumstances or situations will you find a child being abused by his or her biological parents. Most of the cases of loss of self-esteem, self-value and self-image come from their years of growing up, as abuse from people whom they served because their parents didn't have the means and sufficiency to take good care of them and, in the process, were abused. Some were even abused or bullied in schools, some at work at the hands of exploitative employers and some even by their own cruel government.

However, whatever the process through which you got your self-esteem damaged or destroyed, the responsibility lies on you to rebuild, rebrand and restore yourself. One of the major sources of self-abuse is marriage. I have seen so many marriages that have become like a battleground or warfront, as hot and painful as hellfire, where the women are badly abused, molested, devastated and their lives threatened.

The issue of inferiority complex, damaged self-image and loss of self-esteem leads to a lack of self-belief and confidence; and this has become rampant and a force to be reckoned with in our present world. This is so critical because it affects the later parts of many people's lives. Unfortunately, most victims of self-abuse allowed it to degenerate into an inferiority complex, hostility to fellow humans and other forms of crime in society, because they lacked the knowledge and necessary assistance to restore themselves.

No one probably taught them, but it was their responsibility to rebuild their self-esteem, rebrand themselves and consciously restore their self-image. Consequently, they have lived the remainder of their lives in regret, despair, hate, wickedness towards their fellow men, hostility, in fear, self-doubt, failure, discouragement and depression. Most statistical records from different nationalities show that most of the crimes in society today are committed by people who were victims self-abuse in one way or the other in the process of their upbringing, which they could not correct, rebuild, rebrand and restore themselves.

Some found it very shameful and embarrassing to confide in people of the molestations they have gone through, and I thank God most national governments have taken it seriously and as a matter of urgency, and therefore established correction centres where people who have been abused and lost their self-esteem are now being giving attention and assistance. We found much of the cases to be among females; many of them have been victims of rapes, marital abuse and masculine abuse, but today a lot is being done to address the issues such as gender equality and girl-child education campaigns. In this chapter, I shall be addressing some important steps to take to correct, rebuild, rebrand and restore yourself if you are a victim, or know someone who is.

You may not be responsible for all the abuses you have faced and gone through in your life, but it is ultimately your responsibility to see to it that it doesn't affect you psychologically, mentally and emotionally, and that you have to rebuild, rebrand and restore yourself so that ultimately your adulthood will not affected negatively. By the law of childhood upbringing, there are many men today who are abusing their wives or some other women out there, not because it is their nature but because of the abuse that they had to go through when they were young and they grew up with it, and it has ultimately affected the quality of their relationships and lives. They are constituting nuisance in this society and inflicting pain on other people unconsciously, but it doesn't have to be so.

If you were a victim of any form of self-abuse and it has got the better of you, I personally commiserate with you because I understand what it means to be abused, as I had to condone and tolerate the unfair and unjust treatment from people and accepted unpalatable conditions in my own life. However, I thank God I was able to decide to let go of my past and move on to attain the greatness that lies within me and ahead of me, than to allow the past to stop me. I had to let go and fight to become a better me, and today I lead a more quality, rewarding and fulfilling life, my past notwithstanding, and that is the same thing I want for you.

Believe in Yourself

You don't have to let your past stop you; you may not be able to change your past, but you can change your future by taking certain steps and decisions today and now, that will totally rebuild, rebrand and restore you completely. Joyce Meyer was a woman who was morally and sexually abused by her own biological father, but she didn't allow it to stop her; and today she's a global woman of God teaching people all across the nations of the world how to come out of themselves, become their better selves, live worry-free lives, live their best life and rebuild their lives. She has authored many books, including ***Everyday Life***. In the same way, you don't have to let the past stop you, but you can actually use it as platform to reach out to other people so as to make the world a better place for others.

YOUR FUTURE IS WITHIN YOU
The first step in rebuilding, rebranding and restoring yourself in order to bounce back from mistakes, losses, relationship breakups, or from any other pains of the past is to believe that your future is within you. Meaning that there is nothing that you've lost or suffered from that has affected your future, because the future is inside of you, and not outside. This understanding will strengthen you and give you comfort and stability to fight for your dream and restore your self-image and self-esteem.

Philippians 3:13-14.
Brethren, I count not myself to have apprehended: but this one thing I do, forgetting those things which are behind, and reaching forth unto those things which are before, I press toward the mark for the prize of the high calling of God in Christ Jesus.

You have to understand that there is no circumstance or situation of life that you have gone through that had any negative impact on your future, or affected the destiny that lies within you and ahead of you. These experiences have strengthened and equipped you with stamina and wisdom to face the future; you therefore have to thrive to reach for the glory that lies ahead of you.

Your losses, defeats and damages are the things that are behind you and you don't need them in the present or future, so leave them there. What is ahead of you is the prize of working hard to fulfil your dream. Value is within and not without; for instance, no matter how dirty a piece of gold or diamond may look, it hasn't affected its value. If you clean it, the value still remains. The value of most things is trapped within; when a vehicle passes through dirty roads or if someone pours dirty water on your exotic car, or rubs your expensive jewellery in the mud, the dirt on it has not altered its value because the value is found within. All you need to do is clean it up!

YOUR STRENGTH IS WITHIN YOU

Another great asset you have to shape the colour of the destiny you desire or the future that you dream of is your strength, and your strength is within you. Real strength proceeds from within and not from without. With strength, you can achieve anything you want in life; with strength, you overcome the overwhelming challenges and circumstances of your life; with strength, you overcome the oppositions of your life; and, with strength, you can achieve and fulfil your dream. That strength is internal, and true strength springs up from your within.

So, no matter what you have lost, you've not necessarily lost direction because your future is within; your value is within; your greatness is within. Above all, your strength is within you; and it is only when you lose what is within you, such as real virtues like your strength, your vision, or your sound mind, that you've then lost everything. It is with the internal assets that we forge our future and decide the extent to which our lives will shine on Earth for destiny, and life on Earth is unto everyone according to his or her faith or belief.

...According to your faith be it unto you. Matthew 9:29.

> *Life is according to your faith, your destiny is according to your faith, and everything you will ever achieve on Earth is according to your faith.*

Life is according to your faith, your destiny is according to your faith, and everything you will ever achieve on Earth is according to your faith. And your faith is your strength because it strengthens you, it keeps you going in the midst of oppositions and overwhelming circumstances of life; it is the size of your faith that will determine the greatness of your life and the height of your accomplishments.

No one can steal that which is within you; no one can steal your future from you; and no one can steal your destiny. So, get up from the shadow of depression, from the valley of self-contempt and self-doubts; roll up your sleeves and get down to work toward rebuilding, rebranding and restoring yourself.

YOUR FUTURE IS AHEAD OF YOU

One more important truth about you that I would like you to recognise is that your future is ahead of you and never behind you; everything you've gone through is already in the past and not in the future. Everything you've lost, whether relationships, good people, properties or businesses, is nothing compared to the glorious destiny that lies inside and ahead of you. If you understand this, then you will need not worry about whatever you've lost. You are absolutely responsible for the future that lies ahead and within you; and it is in your power to determine what that future will look like by the decisions you make today.

> *What lies inside and ahead of you is incomparable and unquantifiable compared with what you have lost or what is behind you.*

You may not be able to change what has happened in the past, but you can change the outcome of your future by deciding to do things differently today and think differently as well. It is the belief and consciousness, that everything that has happened to you has not affected the future that lies within and ahead of you, that strengthens you to continue in the race of life, despite the trials, in order to attain the dreams that you have always dreamt of. And nothing can ever stop you from achieving your dream, because there is no one that can stop the sun from shining or the moon from giving brightness to the sun.

The same way God did not give any man or woman under the Earth power to control when the sun comes out or when the moon comes out; in the same way, God has not given any man power or authority to control what your future is. When God created you, He created your future as well and no one knows it, no one has seen it, no one can tell it and no one can change it except you. With this consciousness, you are able to clean yourself from the dusts of losses, broken relationships, and pains of the past.

CHANGE YOUR PERCEPTION OF YOURSELF
Believe in your infinite potential. Your only limitations are those you set upon yourself.

Believe in yourself, your abilities and your own potential. Never let self-doubt hold you captive. You are worthy of all that you dream of and hope for.'
— Roy T. Bennett

Another step to rebuilding, rebranding and restoring your self-image and self-esteem is to change the perception of yourself. You see, life is all about perception. Perception has to do with your mental interpretation of the events and circumstances of your life. For example, how do you feel and think about yourself? How do you see things? How do you judge things? And how do you interpret the things that happen to you in relation to your life and destiny? This is so critical and crucial in building a healthy self-image and self-esteem because a lot of negative things will always happen; people will always treat you badly, you will always meet negative people and unjust people who like to do things inappropriately.

You will encounter circumstances and harsh conditions of life, stiff opposition and obstacles that stare you in the face to limit you, but how you interpret all these things will determine the outcome of your life. The way you judge and interpret your broken relationships, losses and other negative events of the past will determine whether you will overcome the past and move towards the greater heights that lie ahead of you, or whether you will be trapped in the abyss of your past and never rise to achieve your dreams.

If you interpret things positively, then you have learnt to differentiate or separate the circumstances of your life from your person. This is so important because your condition is different from you; your condition is just temporary and will go away. It is rather unfortunate that there are many people who take things personally; they have not learnt to differentiate the circumstances of life from their personality. For instance, if someone calls a person negative names or insults them, they see themselves in that light. They get offended and let it get to them. This is wrong! If someone calls you by a name you don't like, that doesn't mean you are that; it just means that is how the person is, because we don't see the world as it is, we see the world as we are.

This implies that, if someone is always seeing negative things in the world, it is evidence that the person himself is full of negativities and that is why everything appears to be negative. Therefore, the prism through which we see life is from our inward perspective and perception of ourselves. When you see yourself as good, you will see that things will be good, because a person is no different from his or her dominant thoughts.

It is crucial to understand that when the perception of yourself changes from negative to positive, from insignificant to significant, from bad to good and from nobody to somebody, then it will result in a corresponding action which will ultimately create the corresponding results. The way you think about yourself sends signals to the external environment and to people who will, in turn, treat you the same way you think about yourself, because your thoughts are always emitting and releasing energy to people. People perceive you the way you think about yourself, because it will always reflect in the way you talk and in the way you behave, and that will in turn influence how people respond and treat you. That is why you must have a healthy image of yourself by changing your perception about yourself.

CHANGING YOUR THOUGHTS

Our thoughts shape our lives and our destiny and that is why you will have to pay attention to the kind of thoughts you entertain in your mind because they will always find practical expression in the physical world. Your thoughts are spiritual entities that carry within themselves spiritual energy that empowers your thoughts to find expression in the external world. Your life is the way it is today because of the thoughts that you predominantly entertain in your heart. According to Charles F. Haanel, 'Man is the sum total of his own thoughts'. He further explains that thoughts are causes and conditions are effects and that is what is responsible for both good and evil. He further explains that thought is creative and will always correlate with its objects because of the cosmological law, which is the law of cause and effect. Therefore, in order to rebuild, rebrand and restore a healthy self-image and self-esteem of yourself, it is crucial that you entertain and sustain the right thoughts in your mind. Until now, many people have not realised the power of thoughts; that thoughts carry mental energies, which are potent enough to translate those thoughts from the mental realm into the physical realm.

Proverbs 23:7, As a man thinketh so is he.

People perceive the way you think about yourself through your words and actions; your thoughts precede your words, your words control your actions, and your action forms your character and attitude, which set the pace of your life and influence how people treat and respond to you. Like I said earlier, it's not just material wealth or riches that attract respect and dignity from people, but the mental interpretation of yourself. It is therefore your responsibility to hold yourself accountable to higher standards on moral attitudes in order to build a good self-image that will attract the right people towards you.

It doesn't matter how bad you've been treated, you should not think of yourself as being a bad person, no matter how many times you have failed. You should not think you are a failure, no matter how many times you've had broken relationships. You should not think or believe that something is wrong with you, or that you are bedevilled; and, no matter how many times you've failed in business, you should never think that you were meant to be poor. You have to change the narratives by changing the way you think, which will, in turn, change the way you speak. That will eventually change the way you act, and your actions are what will change the circumstances of your life. In the words of James Allen, 'We are made or unmade by ourselves. By our thoughts, we forge the weapons by which we can destroy ourselves. Likewise, we also fashion the tools with which we build for ourselves heavenly mansions of joy and strength and peace.'

SET VALUES AND PRINCIPLES TO LIVE BY

Another great step to rebuilding, rebranding and restoring yourself is establishing values and principles for your life by which you may live by. Principles and values set the boundary of your life, they determine the extent to which you will act, what you will do, what you will not do, where you will go, where you will not go, the kind of people to relate with, the kind of businesses to do, the kind of career to pursue and, most importantly, the kind of life partner that you will marry. Principles and values are your watchdog; they protect you from making costly mistakes. I have understood by studying the lives of the great that they are people who live by values and principles and they do everything possible to protect their values and principles. They don't act contrary and they don't break it for anyone.

Making a careful study of my life, I realised that most of the periods in my life when I suffered the most setbacks, hard times, broken relationships and financial losses were when I lived my life without guiding values and principles. I made decisions without paying attention to the kind of destiny I wanted. But I realised not long ago that my principles and values set the limit to what I should do, what I will do, the people I relate with and to whom I will marry and whom I cannot marry. Until you set principles and values for yourself, you may never feel good and great about your personality. Whenever I see myself acting consistently with my principles and values, I feel very special and great about myself. When you let people know that they cannot just walk into and out of your life anyhow, then you will feel a very high level of positivity and greatness about yourself.

Setting boundaries for your actions gives you a very healthy self-image, it makes you think like a champion, it makes you see yourself as a great person. In return, it makes people see you as someone who is great, or who would be great because the world respects people who respect themselves and have self-control and discipline. Setting values and principles to live by gives you a high level of discipline and personal commitment to them, and it will bring you a very great feeling about yourself and positively affect the way you think and act. It will become very obvious for people to see and, in return, you will observe that people will respect you and treat you with dignity and respect.

SETTING PERSONAL GROWTH AND GOAL TARGETS

According to John Maxwell in his book *Leadershift*, he

explains that great leaders have to make a shift from goals to growth; that is, shifting attention from just achieving goals to making personal growth, because it is growth that leads to the achievements or attainment of your goals. This is very correct and I absolutely believe this concept of focusing on growth instead of goal. Setting just a goal can be misleading; it can make you lose or miss the primary thing which is growing. Life is all about growth; in fact, anyone who is not growing is assumed to be dead, because only living things do grow. It is rather appalling to notice that there are many people who just grow in age without growing in wisdom and knowledge.

The fastest and best way to achieve your targets or goals in life is to grow; you have to grow in wisdom, knowledge and understanding in mental capacity and in all ramifications of life in order to achieve your dream. When you grow, you will always achieve goals; achieving your goals is the natural corresponding result of growing, both personally and professionally. Set a target to grow, to become better than you were last month or last year; make it a conscious effort that you will not be where you were the previous year – this is one major key in building a very strong and solid self-image and self-esteem.

> *When you grow and keep growing, you will eventually outgrow your obstacles and limitations*

The successful and great people have a very healthy self-image because success comes with good feelings; it comes with respect and dignity; it comes with a very high and healthy self-image and self-esteem. It makes you see yourself as being significant, a great person, and it makes you see yourself in a positive perspective; and, in order to become successful and great, you need to grow. It therefore means that, at the root of building a healthy self-image and self-esteem, you need to grow from where you used to be to a greater and higher level of knowledge, wisdom and understanding.

PROGRESS ENHANCES YOUR SELF-ESTEEM

You see, when you begin to make some progress in a particular direction you've set for yourself, I can assure you that you will start feeling very special and good about yourself; this is from personal experience. Having achieved some level of personal success, I can tell you that it comes with a great feeling about myself and the more I make one level of progress, the more I want to make a greater progress. In order to do this, I set growth targets that I can easily achieve. Don't set unrealistic targets that you cannot achieve; after a huge loss or failure, I think it's best that you start with setting little targets for yourself, and when you can achieve that you set a higher one as you keep raising the bars of the standard. That is how you keep feeling great about yourself and, like I pointed out earlier, the secret to achieving your targets is to grow.

Make it intentional to hold yourself accountable to a personal life of integrity, honesty, sincerity, courage and personal discipline. These are the forces that make life stronger; these are the building blocks of greatness, and the instruments with which your destiny can be forged. Don't allow people to set disciplines for you; hold yourself accountable to a higher level of discipline than anyone expects or sets for you. If you find yourself working for an organisation, lead your life beyond and above the standard of character, self-discipline and high moral standard that the organisation sets for its employees. By doing so, you are building a strong personal force, resilience and demeanour that radiates from within you and makes you noticeable; it makes your star shine so bright that you cannot be ignored by people – that is a way to build a high self-image and self-esteem for yourself. In the next chapter, I will be addressing the concept of the law of consistent personal development.

MIND YOUR ASSOCIATION

One major factor that was responsible for the damage and loss of my self-image and esteem as a child and teenager was the negative people that were around me. I had so many abusive people in my life, whose method of correcting a child was to abuse and call them negative names, and this affected me psychologically and emotionally. I am aware that many people have similar people around them. In order to rebuild, to rebrand and restore your self-esteem, you have to make it an intentional effort to break away from abusive friendships, abusive relationships and any person that makes you feel bad about yourself.

Whoever talks you down is not qualified to be your friend or to be in the circle of your life; you must be intentional about this, no matter who they are. Whether relatives or family, or colleagues at work, an abusive relationship is toxic; it drains strength, it makes you lose the consciousness of your real self. Never tolerate people that make you feel bad about yourself; don't associate with them; run far away from them, as if you are running away from danger, because they are actually dangerous to your future. Negative words affect and damage self-image and self-esteem, and that is why you have to keep away and break away from anyone that makes you think and feel less of yourself.

DON'T MAKE YOURSELF A 'BEGGAR'

When it comes to relationships, I would advise that, even though I'm not a relationship expert, you keep away or break free from any relationship that puts you on the begging side. You don't have to beg to be in a good relationship, you don't have to beg your friends always to forgive you, you don't have to beg for everything. Actually, begging shows an unhealthy self-image and esteem of yourself. That is something I discovered not so long ago. I actually made a study on the subject of begging and found that, in the Bible from Genesis to Revelation, the word 'begging' appears in three places only:

The first scenario explains the truth that a righteous man is not expected to be a beggar because God is faithful to provide for His own, while the second and the third instances show an

Psalms 37:25; I have been young, and now I am old; yet have I not seen the righteous forsaken, nor his seed begging bread.

Mark 10:46; Blind Bartimaeus, the son of Timaeus, sat by the highway begging,

Luke 18:35; ...a certain blind man sat by the wayside BEGGING.

example of blind men who are begging by the wayside. The question is, are you blind? If you are not, I don't see a reason why you should be begging. Begging is begging, it doesn't matter the circumstances or the situations for which you are begging. The idea of begging makes you lose your self-image, it makes you damage your self-value, because there is nothing good about begging.

I've had relationships where I was always on the begging side. I had to beg the ladies to stay, begged them not to walk away, or begged them to come back. But when this understanding came, I realised the King that I am and my value. Since then, I've never been on the begging side of life and it has greatly enhanced my self-value, self-image and esteem. It is un-kingly to beg, kings don't beg! Great people are not on the begging side of life; they are on the giving side. In a relationship, neither party is doing a favour to the other, it should be mutual.

Both parties should be mutually interested in each other and, therefore, should not warrant one party begging the other. When you do, you are indirectly losing your self-image and self-esteem to the other person. You don't beg for love! Did I say you should not apologise when you offend somebody or your partner? No! By using the word 'please' it's not the same thing as begging. When you say 'please' you are appealing to his or her sense of reasoning and emotion and, at the same time, you are upholding and sustaining your healthy self-image and self-esteem.

BEGGING DIMINISHES YOUR PRESTIGE AND SELF-ESTEEM

Nothing should turn you into a beggar, it is not healthy in building a good self-image and esteem. Don't beg, please! You are worth more than that. If she or he decides to walk away from the relationship, you don't have to beg. Please understand that princes or kings or queens don't beg, and if you see yourself in that light, you will be cautious, respectful and mindful of people's feelings, even without having to beg. It's surprising to discover that there are two major circumstances in life that make people beg: firstly, when you need someone to do you a favour or give you something; and, secondly, when you offend people and need them to forgive you. The Bible didn't tell us to beg in those situations. For instance, in Matthew 7:7 (where we are in need of something from people), Jesus Christ said,

Ask, and it shall be given you; seek, and ye shall find; knock, and it shall be opened unto you.

And Hebrews 4:16 (when we need forgiveness), **Let us come therefore come boldly unto the throne of grace, that we may obtain mercy, and find grace to help in time of need.**

The reason being that God calls us kings, according to **Revelations 5:10, And hast made us unto our God kings and priests: and we shall reign on the earth**.

There is a better way to express your remorse such as, 'Please, I'm sorry, please forgive me' etc. Check out the times that you begged people for one thing or the other, especially when you didn't get what you begged for. Can you remember how you felt? Did it feel good to beg? I remember how I felt; in fact, I could beg at the slightest provocation. I thought it was a sign of humility and being gentlemanly – but I was wrong!

CREATING YOUR IDEAL ENVIRONMENT

Another good step to take in rebuilding, rebranding on

restoring your self-image and esteem is to learn how to create your own ideal environment and live in it most of your time, as it unlocks your genius and potential and makes you a great success in life. By creating your ideal environment, I mean the kind of environment that allows you to maximise your potential, it gives you freedom of expression, it allows you to be your natural self, makes you happy, joyful and puts you at ease all the time. If you can identify the element of such environment, then you can always create it and live in it. In doing that, you will discover that you will naturally succeed without much struggle or effort. For instance, I like the atmosphere of peace, serenity and calmness, and where music plays. I like staying in the presence of God with cool, worship songs, and whenever I want to feel that I am very special, I like to create this kind of atmosphere and, in such an atmosphere, I do great and unimaginable things.

That is where most of my ideas and inspiration come from. I received all my book titles by divine inspiration in such atmospheres, and I write between the hours of 12.00 am to 6.00 am, because I have understood by experience that that period is the most fruitful and productive time of the day for me. As such, I do my best to maximise it. I like my own company and I do everything possible to make sure I'm always in God's presence alone. My life alone is a dwelling place for God. I have literally made my life God's tabernacle, because I have discovered that is the only way I can maximise my potential and become the best of myself.

YOUR IDEAL ENVIRONMENT UNLOCKS YOUR CREATIVITY

I feel most special about myself being alone, enjoying my own company and being alone with God. You have to discover your own ideal environment that unlocks your genius and makes you feel very special, and allows you to express yourself without limitations. I have found that there are very few persons who can make you feel special; there are only a few people whose presence can make you feel great about yourself, without them criticising or making you feel bad.

The world is full of people who are hurting and not happy about themselves, so you won't expect them to make you feel good. We have a lot of negative people in the world, and it's your responsibility to protect yourself from such destructive and negative environments. So, discover your own ideal environment and learn to keep yourself in such an atmosphere most of your time. You don't need people to be special or depend on people's approval to feel special; you can actually make yourself feel special and be special by yourself.

LET IT GO

In order to have a healthy self-image and self-esteem, it is very important to let go of the past and focus on the future that is within and ahead of you. What keeps people down and depressed is their inability to let go of some certain weights and burden in their heart and forgive people who have hurt them, and also forgive themselves for the mistakes they have made. A conscience that is full of pain, regret and offences will make you a slave of your past and destroy the opportunities of the future that lies ahead of you.

There are certain mistakes that people make and find it difficult to forgive themselves for. I've known a lot of people that have made some grievous mistakes in the past, but they have still not found a place in their heart to forgive themselves or to let it go. Some keep bemoaning the past. A good example is one of my close friends whom I would describe as Z. She is a very beautiful and prospective lady; she made a first class degree from the university and was the best graduating student in her department. As a result, the department sent her on a scholarship to Japan for a one-year internship.

Unfortunately, she met a young guy who took advantage of her and defiled her. She is the daughter of high-ranking

Pastor in one of the Eastern states in Nigeria and, as such, she had made a vow to remain a virgin until her wedding night. Unfortunately, the young man manipulated her and defiled her. She came back to Nigeria after her studies so depressed and psychologically traumatised that she was mentally challenged and began to see a psychiatrist because of that. She hated men and everything men represented until I met her.

We became close friends, but her challenge was she couldn't let the past go. She always cried and allowed her past to affect her present – until I decided to help her overcome it. A few times, her siblings would call me, asking me to talk to her so that she would stop weeping and living in self-isolation and depression. She always told me how she had lost her self-esteem and value; she felt that the mistake had taken away her pride and value, and she saw herself as being worthless and depreciated in value.

To cut the story short, I was able to help her come out of that state, within one month of our friendship. She recovered from memory loss, and stopped using the drugs that were prescribed to her by the psychiatrist. The most effective method I used on her was the technique of speaking the right words to her, using affirmations and telling her to always 'Talk herself up', which is the last key I will be sharing in this session. I had to give her Scriptures to read aloud to herself and, most importantly, I made her feel special. She took the responsibility of constantly telling herself how special she was. One time, I had to call her mum to plead with her to talk to her daughter and reassure her always that they were not disappointed in her as her parents, because she always told me her parents were disappointed that she lost her virginity. That was how she rebuilt, rebranded and restored her lost self-esteem and value.

It doesn't matter about your past mistakes or the pain that people have caused you. You must let it go and move on to the promising future with strength, optimism and enthusiasm

Believe in Yourself

in order to take advantage of the opportunities that are ahead. You have to forgive yourself and forgive those who have hurt you deeply; that is the only way you can release yourself from the prison of the past and move gallantly into freedom and limitless possibilities and opportunities that the future presents to you.

> *And herein do I exercise myself, to have always a conscience void of offence toward God, and toward man.*
> *Acts 24:16*

I've known some people in life who are angry not just with man, but also with God. They question God and His existence, they lie against God, saying that He is unjust and partial because of their situations and circumstances, especially when they cannot find the reason behind their predicaments. Some even feel that they have served God, but He has not rewarded them the way they think that God should. They compare themselves with other people who are doing better than they are and they get offended at God. Such attitude is destructive and capable of destroying the future that lies with and ahead of you.

You can't be angry with your maker; you can't be angry with God, and if it is this God that I know, He is faithful, just, gracious and merciful. So, I advise people, whatever the offence and pain that lie in their hearts, to let it go. Forgive yourself, forgive your past and forgive those who have hurt you. Look towards the possibilities of the future, because the future has not been tampered with as it is in you and ahead of you, not behind you!

CREATING A NEW BEGINNING

It is also important to know that it can never be too late to get it right. As long as there is life, there is still hope. You can always get something right, it doesn't matter how long you've been on the wrong path. There are some certain mistakes that can't be corrected and, in such cases, the best thing at that point is to start life afresh, create a new beginning for yourself; a new path for yourself and a new direction that would lead you to an entirely different destination and bring out a new you. It's never too late to start a new life. Start doing the right thing; don't think you've gone too far to turn back from the wrong path, and begin a new life.

There are stories of people who started school very late and graduated in their sixties. There were those who went to school with their children, because they didn't have the opportunity of going to school when they were younger, but that didn't stop them from fulfilling and achieving their goals. There is a chance of starting a new beginning, don't ever think it's too late to start something new. We know the story of the founder of KFC, Colonel Harland Sanders KFC, who started Kentucky Fried Chicken at the age of 62 and, before he died, he became a multimillionaire. You can reinvent yourself by starting something afresh in another direction, to give yourself a different personality and identity from how people used to know you, and through that process you will be able to rebuild, rebrand and restore your self-image and esteem. You can achieve this by changing career or profession, or leaning a new skill to begin something new and different.

TALK YOURSELF UP
The final step I would like to talk about in the process of rebuilding, rebranding and restoring your self-image is to learn to talk yourself up. Have you noticed that most times you felt bad about yourself was simply because of people's disapproval of you, or negative and abusive words spoken at you? Then, how do you change that? If there is nobody to talk good to you, or say positive things to you, why not be the person to approve of yourself and say nice words to yourself? The act of saying positive and good words to yourself is amazing. As ordinary or insignificant as it may appear, in reality it is one of the greatest means of building a healthy self-image. Try being alone and talking to yourself

and you will feel something very special about yourself.

I know this, because I do it all the time. When people say negative things to me or abuse me, especially those who are much older than I am, meaning that I cannot talk back at them, I go back to my closet and begin to tell myself, 'Timothy, you are the best, Tim you are a King, there is no one that is like you. I am special, I am amazing, I am successful, I am great. This world needs me, my generation needs me. I am here to make an impact!' After I have talked to myself, I come out reinvigorated, strengthened from within and passionate about doing great things in life.

I cannot but credit my little successes to my ability to inspire myself, motivate myself and encourage myself, even in times of challenging and overwhelming circumstances of life. I assure you that there will be times when the public will not stand by you; there will be a time when you need to stand alone for what you believe, to defend your convictions, values and what you believe to be right. A time will come when the world will not be on your side and, at that time, you will be your only source of inspiration, motivation, inner strength, courage and confidence. Like I said earlier, your strength is within you, and your sources of strength are the words you speak to yourself always. The Bible says in **Ephesians 5:19,**

…speaking to yourselves in psalms and hymns and spiritual songs, singing and making melody in your heart unto the Lord.

To be honest, I am my greatest company. Many times, I just take myself out and give myself a special treat because I like myself. I love myself and that is why I love my neighbours and humanity. The best way I know to prove to myself that I love myself is to talk to myself, because you naturally love to be around someone you love and always desire to talk to that person all the time. Talking to yourself most of the time is a secret that you need to discover and practise, because it will inspire you and give you inner strength and confidence in the face of challenges.

Don't always expect people to approve of you, praise you or even compliment you before you know you are special or feel special. Do it yourself and for yourself! The world is full of negative people who only see the negative in people instead of the positive; they see weaknesses in people instead of strengths; they see problems in people instead of potentials, failures instead of success, obstacles and limitations instead of opportunities, wrongs instead of rights, and impossibilities instead of possibilities. If you have to depend on these people to make you feel good, you will wait forever; at best, your life will be full of mood swings because, in one minute, somebody will say a good thing about you and, in another, they or someone else will say another thing.

OPRAH WINFREY'S STORY

Oprah Winfrey is an American talk show host, television producer, actress, author, and philanthropist. She was born into poverty and lived with her maternal grandmother, who was chronically poor and couldn't afford good clothes for Winfrey. She wore dresses that were more or less rags, and she was mocked by other children in the neighbourhood because of her terrible state. She was taught how to read at an early age by her grandmother, who took her to church and taught her the Bible. Winfrey learnt how to memorise and recite a lot of the Bible verses and, for this reason, she was nicknamed 'The Preacher'. As a child, she was verbally abused by her abusive grandmother; she eventually went to live with her mother, but there was no room for her and she was evicted, at which point she had to go to her uncle to live with his family.

She suffered from racial prejudice at an early age, and grew up in an environment where children were seen but never heard. At the age of nine, she was sexually abused by her 19-year-old cousin, who also lived with her uncle.

Between the ages of 10 and 14, she suffered more sexual violations, causing her to eventually run out of the house. Unfortunately for her, she became pregnant when she was 14 and made attempts to terminate the pregnancy. She also later attempted suicide, as she had completely lost her self-esteem. It was apparent that her self-image and worth were totally destroyed with the feelings of inferiority complex. She later said that had the internet existed at the time, she probably wouldn't be alive today because she would have just googled how to carry out suicide.

Against all odds, she had to fight adversity to overcome chronic poverty, moving from one family member to another as a kid, always being whipped by her grandmother, ejected from her house, sexually assaulted as a child, suffered an unwanted pregnancy and eventually losing the child, fired from her first job as a news reporter and also experienced racial prejudices. These were all the odds she had to fight when climbing the ranks of the ladder of success to get to the top. Worst of all, she had to fight to rebuild, rebrand and restore her lost and destroyed self-esteem, self-image and self-worth in order to believe in herself and the boundless possibilities that resided within her. In spite of all the things she went through, her potentials were within her, the glorious future was both within her and ahead of her, while her giant was sleeping within her, waiting to be awakened. There is nothing anyone can ever suffer that would deplete one's potentials. It doesn't matter what you have gone through; your future is still within you and ahead of you, so long as you refuse to give up on yourself and fight for your future.

SOME OF HER EXTRAORDINARY ACCOMPLISHMENTS

Oprah Winfrey was the richest African American of the 20th century, North America's first black multibillionaire, and she has been ranked the greatest black philanthropist in American history. By 2007, she was ranked as the most influential woman in the world.

She emerged as a political force in the 2008 presidential race, she endorsed Barack Obama, which was estimated to have been worth about one million votes during the 2008 Democratic primaries in 2013, was awarded the Presidential Medal of Freedom by President Obama and received honorary doctorate degrees from Duke and Harvard in 2008. She is the Chairwoman, CEO and CCO of the Oprah Winfrey Network (OWN). In 1994, she was inducted into the National Women's Hall of Fame, and has a net worth of US$2.7 billion (FORBES Billionaire List 2021) (Source: Oprah Winfrey – Wikipedia).

There's no circumstance you have faced or will ever face that will cancel the reality of the beautiful future that is within you. There is absolutely nothing anyone can do to you that will take away the future that is in you and ahead of you. Instead, everything you will ever go through will serve as a refining fire and production process that will lead to the birthing and fulfilment of your future. The problems and challenges people go through are processes of developing capacity and competencies required to fulfil their destiny, so never give up on yourself for your best days are still ahead of you.

Looking at Oprah's life carefully, it is obvious that she has rebuilt, rebranded and restored her once-lost self-esteem and image and, by studying her path of transformation, you will realise the methods I have listed are consistent with the person she has become today. She is quite influential, she has achieved a lot of her targets or goals, she speaks with power and influence and never talks down to herself because of her past. She has let go of her past and reached forth unto her future. She has created a new beginning, one completely different from what she used to be.

You can also rebuild, rebrand and restore your self-esteem and image if you feel bad about yourself. You could even recommend the process to someone else who is suffering from an inferiority complex and loss of a healthy self-image and esteem.

'There is nothing noble in being superior to your fellow man; true nobility is being superior to your former self.'

—Ernest Hemingway

CHAPTER FOUR
THE POWER OF CONSISTENT SELF-IMPROVEMENT

'Always dream and shoot higher than you know you can do. Do not bother just to be better than your contemporaries or predecessors. Try to be better than yourself.'
—William Faulkner

In this chapter, I will be explaining how to consistently improve and consolidate your self-esteem and image, which has a proportional relationship with your self-belief and confidence. One of the key factors to achieving this is continuously practising the principle of personal development. This principle has become very popular and widely used, even among major corporations and especially global organisations; they have come to realise the importance of consistently developing their workforce to be equipped with the necessary competences and skills required to achieve maximum effectiveness in the workplace. The importance of this principle cannot be over emphasised, as it is the key to growth and sustainability in any industry or corridor of endeavour.

The major way in which organisations achieve their goals and objectives is by consistently investing in their priceless assets, which is the workforce. The workforce of any organisation is the greatest asset in achieving their corporate missions and visions; without this, they will be defeated in the markets by their competitors. So, as customer needs are ever changing and increasing, and with the increasing dynamics of the business markets, it has become imperative and pertinent for organisations to consistently invest in their workforce to improve their effectiveness and efficiency, because the employees are their greatest assets in driving change and achieving the organisational goals and objectives.

CHANGE IS CONSTANT AND SWIFT

As human needs change and with the rapid and increasing dynamics in human behaviour, anyone who must succeed in this 21st century, and present times of change and uncertainties, must consistently take responsibility for improving and updating his or her self through the principle of consistent personal development. It has to be consistent and intentional, because change is constant and takes place swiftly. The techniques and ideas that worked yesterday would become obsolete today. The rate of obsolescence in our world today is so fast that, without conscious and intentional efforts towards improving yourself, you'll be left behind by civilisation. Unfortunately, there are many people in this age that are behind civilisation; some people are still operating with outdated knowledge and information and that is why they struggle in businesses, human relationships and in virtually every aspect of their lives.

In order to succeed and be relevant in these times, you must keep abreast with the constant changes around your environment and in your industry or field; and the best and probably the only way to do this is to personally invest in yourself and consistently improve your knowledge, skills and competence so that you remain competitive in this competitive world. The world has become so competitive, the competitiveness in the marketplace is very stiff and fierce, that only those who are prepared will survive. It has become like the survival of the fittest because, every day, things are changing, innovations are coming in, new ideas are springing up, and people – and especially your competitors – are coming up with better ideas to outsmart you and, if you do nothing about it, you will become redundant and outdated and your place will be taken over by those who know better than you because they are consistently making improvements in themselves.

CHANGE IS INEVITABLE

This principle is so crucial in these times of change. In this 21st century, many previous ideas and techniques are no longer working and new things are being introduced every day; therefore, the only way to be relevant and measure up is to make sure you keep with growth and development in your industry and profession.

Both knowledge and skills easily become outdated. For instance, if your skill was necessary in one particular field and there is a need for you to change into another field because of the dynamics and complexity of the marketplace, it therefore requires that you also have to update your skills. Therefore, to be relevant we must consistently assess and analyse ourselves to determine whether we are consistent with the change and demands in our workplace and environments where we find ourselves. It is also important to know that you might be competent in one area, but incompetent in other areas or new horizon you would need to explore; in such a case, you have to carry out a self-assessment and analysis of the skills and competences that will be required in order to function effectively and compete favourably in the new place.

One thing is certain, and that is that change happens. The only thing that is constant is change, and for you to keep up with change in society and the workplace you must keep changing, and the key to changing is to adopt the principle of consistent self-improvement.

We live in uncertain times and in a fast-changing world, and for you to be relevant you have to consistently seek personal and professional changes that are consistent with the changes in our present time. If you refuse to change by yourself, you will inevitably be forced to change by the changes taking place around you in the business world or marketplace. Never in the history of the world has man ever lived in such uncertain and fast-changing times as our present generation, a fast-world generation, fast-food generation and fast-everything generation. The future is so uncertain and the only way to predict the future is to create it by repositioning yourself to become relevant in the future, and the only way to achieve this is by way of change and personal development.

CONSISTENT INCREMENTAL SUCCESS BOOSTS SELF-IMAGE AND ESTEEM

Consistent and incremental personal success enhances and consolidates your self-image, self-value esteem, self-belief and confidence. Making consistent incremental progress or success has a huge positive impact on you and the way you feel about yourself; it makes you feel good and special and it makes you feel very positive and enthusiastic. Making incremental improvements in yourself and your career has a way of positively influencing the way you see yourself – which is your self-image and esteem. If you meet successful people who have been able to accomplish some level of business success in their lives, you will always observe that they exude a very high level of self-confidence; they feel so proud about themselves, they are very enthusiastic and optimistic and always looking forward to the next Success.

You always see them walk with their shoulders high. It is not pride or arrogance, it's just the normal by-product of self-improvement and progress in your profession. Setting goals and achieving them makes you feel great about yourself, it makes you believe that you can, it makes you believe in possibilities, it enhances your confidence level and increases your self-confidence. It helps you to question your doubts and fears and conquer every limiting obstacle on your way.

BE COMMITTED TO LIFELONG LEARNING

'No matter who you are, no matter what you did, no matter where you've come from, you can always change, become a better version of yourself.'

— Madonna

THE POWER OF CONSISTENT SELF-IMPROVEMENT

Learning is the key to self-improvement and self-improvement is the key to growth, and growth is the key to achieving your goals and objectives. You can see the chain of network or interconnectivity. Like I discussed earlier, growing is the key to achieving your goals and, in order to grow, you must give yourself to a lifestyle of consistent personal improvement or development. To consistently reinforce and consolidate your self-belief level, your confidence level, and self-esteem and image, you must always think of ways of making intentional efforts towards progressing and advancing from one level of success to another, and you can only achieve that if you ae committed to lifelong learning. Life is designed to be progressive; not to be static. Whenever you observe or notice stagnation in your life, or if you are being static for a long period of time, it could possibly and probably be an indication that your current skills, knowledge and competences have become obsolete and can no longer enable you to achieve your goals and objectives; at such a crossroad, you need to assess and analyse yourself for any gaps in yourself towards achieving progress.

> *It is normal to be progressive, but abnormal to be stagnated.*

Consistent self-assessment and analysis to discover the gaps in your skills and competences is a major way to consistently improve yourself, because it will point you to the necessary skills and competences that you lack, but which you need to move from where you currently are to where you need to be. This is why the principle of personal improvement is crucial.

Life is progressive and so you should thrive to be progressive, too. In the words of Martin Luther King Jnr., if you cannot fly, run, if you cannot run, walk, and if you cannot walk, crawl. But by all means make sure you keep moving. Stagnated

> *Martin Luther King Jnr., if you cannot fly, run, if you cannot run, walk, and if you cannot walk, crawl. But by all means make sure you keep moving.*

people never feel good about themselves, unsuccessful people are never proud of themselves, and mediocre and ordinary people have never been proud of themselves because there is nothing to be proud about being a failure and being poor.

I've never seen a successful or a great man who does not have a healthy self-image, high self-esteem, and high level of self-confidence, except for when they feel guilty that the source of their success is through dishonest and inappropriate means. Truly, success begins with the mental disposition that you can succeed against all odds. It begins with the right mental perception, the right thoughts and the right attitude that you can make a difference in life.

SUCCESS COMMANDS ATTENTION
Success and greatness attract people to you, it earns you self-respect and dignity among peers and the general public, it commands attention and naturally draws people to you. If you want to be distinguished from the crowd and walk with a high level of power and confidence, then leading a successful and progressive life must be your goal, and you cannot achieve this if you are not consistently investing in yourself. This is a principle that drives change, excellence and effectiveness in everything you will ever do.

SUCCESS HAS DEMANDS
No one has ever accomplished a great thing in life by chance or accident; greatness is a conscious effort and success is intentional as well. Whenever you see someone do a great thing, or do something that has never been done before, then it is proof that someone dared believed in himself and in his capability and potentials. Nobody becomes a star by chance, nobody becomes great by wishing, and no one achieves a very high level of personal success and greatness by mistake. Achievement and success are all by-products

Achievement and success are all by-products of a high degree of belief in one's self

of a high degree of belief in one's self; your desire to excel and make a difference in life will always require you to believe in yourself and have a high level of self-esteem and self-image.

> *No price is too much to pay if it absolutely guarantees your success, happiness and fulfilment in life*

One very important question you will always have to ask yourself periodically is: What do I need to do to get to where I desire to be? Or, what does it take to get to the next level that I desire in life? Success has a demand; it is a good thing to desire to be successful, but it comes with responsibility. Greatness has demands, achievement has demands, your goals and objectives have demands, and everything you will want to achieve in life will definitely make a demand on you. I often say, ***no price is too much to pay if it absolutely guarantees your success.*** There is always a price to pay and you have to always ask: What do I have to do now to get to the next level, that I desire to be tomorrow? The second question you have to always ask is: Do I currently have what it takes to achieve my goals and objectives, or to take me from where I am now to where I desire to be?

CONSISTENT SELF-IMPROVEMENT IS KEY TO LIFE TRANSFORMATION

'Things do not grow better; they remain as they are. It is we who grow better, by the changes we make in ourselves.'
— Swami Vivekananda

It doesn't matter what anyone's current level or status is in life, as it can be turned around through the principle of consistent self-improvement. But how does this happen? What is the process through which life is transformed by self-improvement? How do you apply

> *An attitude of consistent self-improvement is the key and secret to life transformation.*

this principle of consistent self-improvement in order to transform your life? That is what I will be addressing in the next chapter through the model I developed. I just need you to understand that this is one singular key that will transform your life around and give you a strong and healthy self-image and prestige. As it has been said, 'You will remain the same person you are and at the same place in the next five years except for two reasons: your association and the books you read, because these are the two major processes of getting information and it's the quality of the information you consume that determines the quality of your life.

The process of self-improvement is mind transformation. True and genuine changes take place in the mind and then manifest in the external. Lasting changes and transformation must begin from within, internal, or in your mind before they manifest in the physical, just like a woman must first conceive a child in her womb before the physical birth after nine months. Whatever hasn't been conceived in the mind, any change that didn't begin within the mind will not last. That is why we read in the Bible that **Be ye transformed by the renewing of your mind. Romans 12:2**

'Formal education will make you a living; self-education will make you a fortune.'

—Jim Rohn

CHAPTER FIVE
THE PROCESS OF LIFE TRANSFORMATION

'Those who cannot change their minds cannot change anything.'
—George Bernard Shaw

So many writers have written books on the subject of consistent self-improvement, popularly known as the principle of personal development programme, but only a handful of writers have explained the process to help people apply it in their own lives. If you know the reason (the 'why') for doing something, you will always find the ways (the 'how') to accomplish it. Many people get bored and give up in the process of doing something simply because they don't have enough 'whys' or reasons for doing it. If you can find a good 'why' for something you want to accomplish, then you will always find the ways to do it.

I have read several books and attended some seminars on the subject of personal development programme, or self-improvement, but didn't give it serious commitment because probably I was not told the reason to do it – and, of course, there was little passion to find the ways and process of its application in my life, and I know that many people out there are facing a similar situation. If people cannot find enough reasons or the 'why' for the cost of an action, they will give up along the way because they won't have sufficient drive or passion to sustain them in order to accomplish what they desired initially.

However, it is not enough to know the 'why' or the reasons to do something; it is also very important to know the means and 'how' to do it. For instance, if someone tells you why you need a particular product but cannot tell you how to access it, then there is no need because eventually it will not benefit you. It is not enough to know that there is a particular product or service that will satisfy your need, but it is also very important to know how to access it. Knowing all the reasons or importance of something, but not knowing how to achieve it, can be frustrating.

There are many people talking about the principle of consistent self-improvement and personal development programme, but just a handful of people will tell you how to do it. In this chapter, I will be sharing with you a simple model that I developed that will teach you how to apply the principle of consistent self-improvement to your life. It is a simple model, but very effective and powerful in application.

THE NEXT IDENTITY MODEL

This is a simple and highly effective tool or process of life transformation that I developed in order to help people transform their lives and become the person they have always dreamt of, and teaches how to move your life from where you currently are to where you desire to be in the future. It connects you from your present position to where you wish to be tomorrow. It is very effective and yet very simple to understand and apply. It is based on the concept of 'Same Person, Different Identity'. It explains the fact that everyone has different identities but that, in order to transform yourself from your current identity to the next, there is a price to be paid, which is known as the 'Process of Transformation'.

To illustrate this better, take yourself for example. When you were born, there was an identity that you had; after 10 years, you had another identity, but were still the same person, and after 10 years again you had another identity, yet you were still the same person, and after 10 years again you (will) still have another identity, but will still be the same person that you are, and it continues until you eventually die. So, this model explains how to break your life into segments of years, where you segment your life into a range of years suitable to you, because people are different and are faced with different challenges, different governments and economies, and their rate of growth is different.

I suggest segmenting your life into decades to enable you to accommodate all the changes necessary to transit into another phase of life. A decade is long enough to make considerable changes and progress, both personally and professionally, so I advise you break the phases of your life into decades. This implies that you make long-term goals, whereby every decade you will definitely make a giant stride, accomplish a milestone and transit into another new phase of your life and career.

There are some parts of the world where a child of 5-7 years may be in secondary school because of their environmental and economic factors that aid rapid growth, while in other parts of the world the rate of growth or child's development may be very slow; you may see a child of 10 years still in primary school. Therefore, it doesn't matter where you are or what the factors or rate of growth and development are, you can still use this model and apply it very effectively to suit your own process of growth. In order words, set it at your own pace and you will still achieve the goal. Remember what I said in the first chapter, that self-belief helps you become yourself.

COMPETING WITH YOURSELF; BEATING YOUR PREVIOUS PERFORMANCE

This book is all about you and not another person. You have to personalise it to get the best out of it, as **the first law of self-belief 'is never to compare yourself with another person'.** The best type of competition is self-competition; it's the type of competition that helps you beat your previous performance, not another person's performance. Think of how to beat your previous accomplishment, how to

The first law of self-belief 'is never to compare yourself with another person'

become better than you were the previous month or year, how to outperform yourself and not others. Thinking this way will make you put things into perspective that you are your own enemy or friend.

The importance of this thought pattern is that it will inspire you to beat your last performance, to do better, and to improve. There is no limit to improvement and excellence in life. We are inelastic, the human mind is inelastic, so you can keep stretching and improving yourself indefinitely. Let us take, for instance, that a student scored 80 in his class which is an 'A', and perhaps was the highest score in his class of 25; by applying this concept of outperforming your previous self or record, he or she decides to make above 80 next time, and if he continues until he gets to 100, being the maximum score, he could still decide to focus on the aspect of the time it takes him to finish an exam or read the material. He may say, 'It took me one hour to achieve that, next time I will use fifty minutes to do the same thing.' That is also an example of improving your efficiency.

The ultimate benefit of this is that, as you keep outperforming your last performance and becoming better than you were previously, a time will come when you will be the best in your field of career. You will become the most outstanding, the most successful and the most exceptional. But you didn't achieve that by focusing on someone else, or trying to beat or break someone else's record; you achieved that success by competing with and against your own self.

Another important aspect of self-competition is that you have no one to envy, or to hate, or to contend or strive with, which is the major reason behind conflicts, disagreement and unhealthy rivalries among people in the same sphere of business or career.

The simple diagram below shows the next identity model.

Next Identity Model (Same person, Different Identities)

FIGURE 1

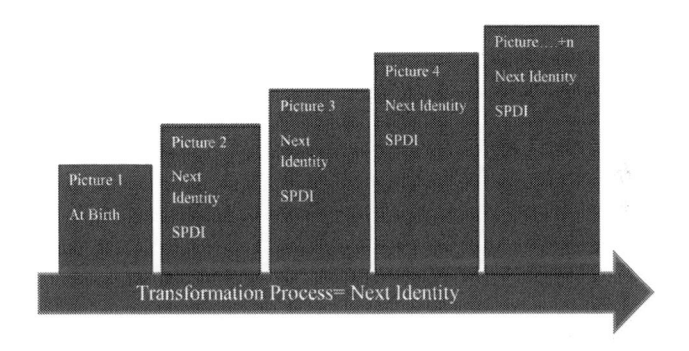

The SPDI stands for 'Same Person Different Identity' and it is on this premise that this model works. It connects your present to your future, it is a model that shows your target(vision, goal or objectives), tells you where you are per time, and also shows you how to get to where you desire to be in the future. Like I said, the 'How' is as important as the 'Why' because, without the 'How' to get there, your reasons or targets will never be met.

No matter the accuracy of the vision or how great your ideas are, if you don't know the 'How' to turn it into reality, it could lead to depression and discouragement. The major reason behind most unsuccessful and unhappy people in the world today is not a bankruptcy of ideas or lack of potentials and talents, but primarily because they lack the knowledge of

The labour of the foolish wearieth every one of them, because he knoweth not how to go to the city. Ecclesiastes 10:15

how to achieve their dreams. If they knew how to do the business or work out their ideas and translate them into reality, many of these people would be among the world's richest men/women today. But lack of the 'How Factor' has been responsible for many people's failure.

What factors are responsible for the Next Identities? What factors are responsible for the changes in the identity of a person in the next identity model? It is the transformation process.

The Transformation Process: this represents the factors that are responsible for moving you from where you currently are to where you desire to be, they determine the degree of the transformation and changes that take place in your life in order to change your identity. Whether you will succeed or not, whether you will achieve your targets and goals or not, will depend on these factors. They lead to your change and transformation and that is where you need to pay attention if you wish to come out with a new identity.

The 'Transformation Processes' you go through in life will determine your next identities. The major factor responsible for your transformation process is consistent self-improvement, and the factors of self-improvement and development are reading, right association, lifelong learning, learning new skills, acquiring new information, right attitude, changing your perception and mental disposition or beliefs, the pains and experiences you go through in life, lessons that life pains teach you, believing in yourself, carrying the 'I can' consciousness, stretching yourself beyond your limits, stepping into new horizons, and things like these. All the efforts you put into your life and career to enhance your life are the factors that create your transformation, and your level of transformation creates your new or next identity.

If you determine or decide the kind of identity you desire to have, then it will inform the kind or quality of transformation you need to go through. Imagine the level of transformation an SMEs entrepreneur, who desires to transit his business from his local domain or confinement into a global conglomerate, will have to go through? The demands of starting up an SME and running it just within the entrepreneur's locality will be little compared to when he desires to transit into a multinational corporation. He will need to do a lot of market research, discover the best method to penetrate the international market, he will think of the cultural and political climates of different nations and what kind of products to introduce and, of course, the manpower resources and personnel.

So, every form of new identity you desire will demand one level of transformation and, until you able to meet such demand of transformation, you will never have a change of identity and achieve your targets. Another example is a governor who decides to ascend the seat of the presidency; it requires much greater efforts because the challenge of leading a state is little compared to that of leading a whole nation. In his or her campaign for the presidency, he or she will likely need to visit almost all the states within the nation to canvass for their votes and, in each case, must have to tailor his or her speeches to satisfy their perspectives and aspirations to win their mandates.

GROWTH NOT GOALS

The key to your next identity is to determine the kind of a personality (identity) you desire and put yourself through the process of transformation required. However, it is good to understand that transformation is cumulative; as you keep investing into yourself, there will be a measure of invisible or intangible incremental progressions and changes taking place within; this will continue until it accumulates into a greater and tangible transformation within that will lead to some major accomplishments or progress in the physical. How do you know you are consistently growing? Your proof of transformation is firstly the quality of life you lead, your relationship with people improves, your character and attitude change positively, you are becoming a better you than you were, you observe a radical transformation in the quality of life you lead. This is the most important benefit of life transformation, not Results or Goals attainment, because a good name is better than riches. '

It is rather misleading that many people have defined success or greatness to be all about results and goals attainment. Although those things are good, they are not the ultimate test of a great, rewarding, fulfilling and transformed life. Results don't necessarily indicate you are growing; material gains, riches and wealth are not proof of a quality and transformed life, because there are billionaire looters of national treasuries, corrupt rich men and women, corrupt politicians, rich fraudsters, criminals, kidnappers, and all kinds of bad sources of money. There is good and bad success!

So, when talking about the major evidence of growth and transformation, I am first referring to results in the quality of life one leads, such as a life of integrity and honesty, better relationships with others, especially in marital relationships and family, love for mankind, the influence and impact you make in the lives of people around you – and, of course, you don't have to be rich to influence someone's life positively. Secondly, it will also show in the attainment and achievements of your goals and targets in your career and profession.

TIM OPARAJI'S SUCCESS MODEL (TOPS MODEL)

In my study of successful men and women, both past and present, and in trying to unravel the reason behind advancement in life, scientific development and inventions, successful accomplishments of great feats, and also the failures of most people on planet Earth, I came up with what I call the **'TOPS MODEL'**. It is a model I developed over many years during my quest to discover the reasons for success and failure. It gives vivid explanations to all these various events as mentioned above. More importantly, it also proves my claim or perspective that *nothing is actually 'impossible'* and the Holy Bible also states this very clearly.

"(Jesus said unto him, If thou can believe, all things are POSSIBLE to him that BELIEVES. Mark 9:23)"

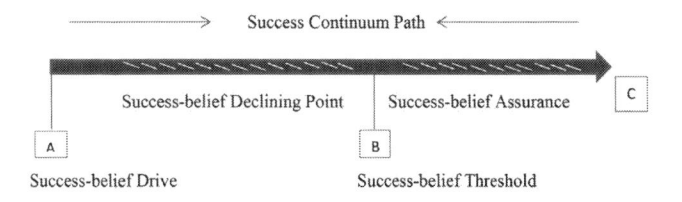

Fig.2   Tim Oparaji's Success Model (TOPS MODEL)

The various points are as follows:
1. Success-Continuum Path (SCP)
2. Success-belief Drive (SBD)
3. Success-belief Declining Point (SBDP)
4. Success-belief Threshold (SBT)
5. Success-belief Conviction (SBC)

SUCCESS-CONTINUUM PATH
The thick, straight line is the Success-Continuum Path, which represents the path of success towards the accomplishment of any feat, whether in scientific research, quest for invention, innovation, excellence, mining of mineral resources beneath the Earth's surface, spiritual adventure, or search for success in any area or aspect of human endeavour. The Success-Continuum Path represents the path to the success you desire and seek.

SUCCESS-BELIEF DRIVE
The success-belief drive is the desire or drive for success, the need or desire to succeed or achieve a particular goal. You could also call it your Passion for Success. Actually, the beginning of every accomplishment or success is the desire and drive to achieve something and make a difference; the

need to make a contribution, which is what usually drives every individual towards a specific path of progress and success in any human endeavour. A sportsman has a drive to become the best sportsman, whether in football or other areas of sport, the scientist has a desire and drive to make some discoveries and inventions, etc. It all begins with a drive and passion to excel in something.

SUCCESS-BELIEF DECLINING POINT

This is a point along the Success-Continuum Path where the person's drive or passion for success begins to drop or decline due to many factors such as discouragement, impatience, fears, self-doubts, oppositions, lack of resilience, distractions and critics. Usually, most people begin with a high zeal, success drive or passion, high expectations; some even assume they will succeed without resistance and, in the face of oppositions, their success drive begins to decline until it gets to a point where they give up.

The most common factor behind this is a lack of persistence. Most times, the most singular factor of success will be the 'staying power' or ability to persevere and persist in the face of obstacles and oppositions. It is sad to know that many people have given up just steps away from their breakthrough point. For instance, I read a story in the book, *Think and Grow Rich* by Napoleon Hill, about a man who had a piece of land and had to dig it in search of oil; but after a long while of digging without hitting any oil deposit, he got discouraged and gave up and sold the land to another person. This new owner continued from where this man stopped and, after just one strike, behold – oil gushed out and he became a billionaire overnight.

'Most times, what people need to excel is not more talents, gifts, knowledge, wisdom or power but perseverance and persistence.'

If you would just persevere and hang on in there, you will succeed. This is the major reason for most of the failures of human kind. My big brother, who sponsored me to go to the UK to study for my masters, always told me these words:

He is a self-made billionaire who had a humbling background and had to fight his way to the top. He always encouraged me to fight for my future and create my own opportunities; in the midst of my challenges, he always comes to cheer me up with wisdom and inspirational words such as, 'challenges are normal', 'no one great today had it smooth', 'don't give up'.

> *'Keep pushing, there is no space anywhere, it is people that create their own space in life.'— Pastor Chijioke Okonkwo*

His constant words of advice to me always are 'keep pushing'. I believe this is one great secret to success.

SUCCESS-BELIEF THRESHOLD

This is the measure of self-belief and success-drive sufficient enough to take you beyond all forms of oppositions, challenges, limitations, obstacles and discouragements along the line of the Success-Continuum Path to achieve your goals and targets. It is the point where your expectations and dreams become your reality; it is the measure of faith and success drive that can never be subdued and quenched by your fears and doubts; it is at this point you hit your targets and achieve your pursuits. There will always be limitations and oppositions that stand in the way of success (Success-Continuum Path) to stop you, and it is because of these forces of oppositions that most people lose hope and suddenly their success drive begins to decline, until they eventually give up and quit. That is why we have so many poor and unsuccessful people in the world.

There is nothing as terrible as men of potentials and talents but who are highly unsuccessful; the world is filled with such people in every corner and race. It is not just ideas, talents and potentials that are primarily responsible for success in life. In fact, most successful and outstanding people in life are not as talented and gifted as those unsuccessful ones, because it doesn't just take talents, potentials and gifts to excel in life. There are many poor people with great ideas, talents and potentials, but the problem is primarily their inability to persevere and persist in the face of overwhelming challenges and oppositions until they succeed.

They just lack the willpower and discipline to hang on. But, if you must succeed, your success-belief threshold must be very high in order to stay strong through the obstacles and oppositions you will meet. For instance, the great inventor of our time, Thomas Edison, failed over 10,000 times in his attempt to discover the incandescent bulb before he succeeded, but he never gave up because his success drive was very high and strong enough to take him past the discouragements and disappointments he met along the Success-Continuum path. When asked by a reporter, 'How did you feel after failing 10,000 times?' Edison simply replied, 'I didn't fail 10,000 times. I only discovered 10,000 wrong ways the bulb couldn't have been invented.' Also, Albert Einstein met with many failed attempts in his quest for success, but that didn't deter or drain his success drive. He said, 'I have tried 99 times and have failed, but on the 100th time came success.'

SUCCESS-BELIEF CONVICTION

This is actually the realm of solid faith and absolute conviction in your ability or resolve to succeed against all odds. When you start out with any endeavour that, no matter what it takes, you will never give up; then you will always succeed because it is unto every man according to his believe. It is a zone of rest and assurance whereby you believe that you are able to overcome every challenge and obstacles that stands in your way to success. Having such a mindset will always take you above the limitations and obstacles in life. Actually, it is your mentality and consciousness that usually lift you above the oppositions and obstacles that will come your way. The fact is, they will always come, but the question is, 'Is your faith, success drive and passion strong enough to overcome all those things and see beyond the present challenges and limitations into the great future, goals and targets that you desire?'

If you have this kind of conviction, it will infuse rest, peace and stability in you, no matter what comes your way. Such a conviction is the trading capital of champions in life. This is the trading capital that great men use to trade in the realms of life. When you see an ordinary man doing extraordinary things, it is not necessarily because they are extraordinary or a superhuman being, it's just that they have unwavering, unstaggered and unstoppable faith and conviction in themselves, that even if the whole world is against them, they cannot be stopped or subdued. And, with such strong faith and conviction, nothing can ever stop you from achieving your quests.

NOTHING IS ACTUALLY IMPOSSIBLE
The Success Model proves my position that nothing is actually impossible in this life. It is a measure of your Success-Belief Drive that determines if something is achievable or not. In my own opinion, the word impossible should not be a term that should be used when it has to do with a quest for success and accomplishments. In reality, there is nothing impossible; it is the measure of our competency, commitment, capacity or ability that determines if something will be achievable or not. If someone's competency, capacity or ability is insufficient to do something, that doesn't make that thing an impossible task, it just means that the person lacks sufficient capacity, knowledge, experience or ability to get it done.

The word impossible is just a term that people unconsciously use to describe or refer to something that they are not able to do; and, more so, if someone is unable to do something, it does not mean that there is no one in the world that can do such a thing. It's also important to take into cognizance that when it comes to achievements, time is also of paramount importance because, with the passage of time, new dispensations are unfolded and things will become

Believe in Yourself

increasingly easier because of the increment and abundance of information, knowledge, development of more skills and competences, and dynamics of human abilities. In the medieval age, things like aeroplanes, computers, telephones and all the electrical and sophisticated gadgets that are used today were not available to the people, because the people of those generations lacked the competences, skills, capacity, knowledge, intelligence, expertise and the ability to do those things. However, that didn't mean that those things were impossible. It is good to separate these two scenarios, as they are not the same; in most cases, it is usually the case of someone lacking the ability and capacity to do something and not a case of 'impossibility'.

What could not be done in the past generations are now possible in this generation; and, subsequently, the challenges of the present time that will not be solved in this present generation would eventually become possible in succeeding generations because of the progress of time that leads to an increase in knowledge, information and development of better competences and skills. Therefore, instead of thinking something is impossible, it is better to shift the focus and think of ways to enhance and increase your abilities and capacity to do something. It is someone's capacity, knowledge and ability that will eventually determine what can be done or not.

THREE FEET FROM GOLD

In his all-time classic book, *Think and Grow Rich*, Napoleon Hill tells the story of R. U. Darby. The uncle of R. U. Darby was obsessed with the desire and passion to find gold, so he staked his claim and actually went digging for gold, and eventually found gold ore after several weeks of hard labour and consistency. Upon realising he didn't have the machinery to extract the gold ore, he left it and went to his family to raise some money to acquire the equipment needed to explore the gold ore. Eventually, Darby and his uncle were able to raise a substantiable amount of money with which he acquired the needed equipment, and both of them returned to the mine to continue with the exploration.

They began to explore and accumulated a good quantity of gold ore. Darby and his uncle were very happy as everything was going according to expectations, when suddenly the wind of fortune blew in a contrary direction, and the flow of gold ore ceased. They kept digging and, after a long while, they became exhausted and fed up, and consequently they threw in the towel. Out of frustration, they sold their equipment to a junk man for some hundred dollars.

After they departed in frustration and disappointment, the junk man sought for professional advice from a mining engineer to inspect the mine. He investigated the mine and discovered that there was a vein of gold just THREE FEET from the point where Darby and his uncle had given up and stopped digging. Consequently, he made millions from the mining.

This story is a perfect example that substantiates the truth that nothing is actually impossible, that people give up before meeting with success and so they term their situation an impossible case. Most people failed in life because they didn't have the convictions, persistence and perseverance required to overturn the temporary defeats and obstacles that stood in their way. Darby and his uncle gave up because of two reasons: lack of adequate information or knowledge, and lack of persistence to dig three feet deeper where the gold ore was. This is the case with so many scenarios that people call impossible; having tried something for several years without success still doesn't justify it as impossible. There are many factors that could be responsible and, until you have exhausted all options, you can't call something impossible.

You may ask, 'Tim, how long should I exercise persistence and perseverance in order to meet with success?' Well, the answer is, 'If you are sure you have the right information and adequate knowledge, strategy and tactics, then you will have to persist and persevere till you succeed. It varies depending on what task you seek to accomplish. It may take hours, days, weeks, months or even years, but by all means, keep at it until you succeed.' Without doubt, if you are expending efforts and resources in the wrong direction, without adequate knowledge and the right information, you will not succeed.

There is no bad or good idea, it's your attitude that makes an idea a great one.

There is no bad idea or good idea, it's your attitude that makes an idea a great one. Ideas don't fail because they are bad, but because of insufficient knowledge, lack of correct information, poor planning, strategy and tactics and lack of competency and capacity to turn it into reality. That same idea that you think is absurd, sell it to someone else who knows what to do, you will be surprised by the success they will make out of it. The Bible clearly states that knowing what to do is a key to achieving your goal,

The labour of the foolish wearieth every one of them, because he knoweth not how to go to the city. Ecclesiastes 10:15

The problem is that many people don't know what to do and, even if they know, many still don't know how to do it, which is the most important factor that translates ideas into success, and that is why partnership and collaboration is a great business strategy. What you don't know can be complimented by another's expertise and competency. Building a formidable team with diverse competencies is a great key to success, as you can't accomplish much by working as a one-man team. There is always a way out of every problem and challenge of life, and the primary thing I want you to get from this book is that nothing is impossible. You might not discover the way to do something, or a solution to a major problem you are trying to solve, or how to accomplish a particular thing. I can assure you that it's not a case of impossibility, but knowledge-based, capacity-based, competence-based, strategy and tactics-based, persistence-based, and perseverance-based.

In summary, I wish to submit that impossibility or possibility are just terms that most people unconsciously use to refer to our measure of persistence, endurance, convictions, capacity, competence, ability, information or knowledge to either do something or not; and not necessarily because anything is impossible. Possibility or impossibility is, therefore, competency-based, capacity-based, intelligence-based, perseverance-based, persistence-based, knowledge-based, information-based and success-drive-based and, most importantly, time-based, dispensation-based or generation-based. The extent or degree to which we will be willing to sustain our success-drive or passion to succeed against all the odds is what will define what will be possible to us or impossible to us. As the Bible rightly says,

Ideas don't fail because they are bad, but because of insufficient knowledge, lack of correct information, poor planning, strategy and tactics and lack of competency and capacity to turn it into reality

Jesus said unto him, if thou canst believe, ALL THINGS are POSSIBLE to him that BELIEVETH. Mark 9:23

And the wise Apostle Paul said,

**'I can do all things through Christ which strengthens me...
Philippians 4:14**

This doesn't in any way connote 'impossibility'.

This clearly substantiates my claim that *possibility or impossibility is competency-based and based on other various human factors, especially our belief which is Success-Belief Drive.*

This is the model that clearly explains all of humankind's development, achievements, breakthroughs, successes and advancements in all fields of human endeavours, as well as failures, to achieve anything.

'Men do not shape destiny, Destiny produces the man for the hour.'
—**Fidel Castro**

CHAPTER SIX
DESTINY IS CALLING

'A man does not make his destiny: he accepts it or denies it.'
—Ursula K. Le Guin

There is a call of destiny waiting for everyone to answer and, until you answer that call of destiny, you might never be fulfilled in life. It is good to put into perspective how success or progress in life is different from fulfilment. They mean absolutely different things; one can be financially prosperous and successful, yet unhappy, unsatisfied and unfulfilled because fulfilment has to do with filling the inner vacuum in man, and the only way to fulfil that inner yearning and vacuum is by answering the call of Destiny.

There is a place called Destiny and that is where your greatness and fulfilment will come from. Every day on the pages of newspapers and headlines news across the world, we hear sad stories of people who commit suicide, including the financially successful. In the United Kingdom, a nation of great advancement and prosperity, the cases of depression and suicide have become a force to be reckoned with.

The government makes adequate provisions and supplies to her citizens, even the unemployed have access to government funding and support, but that hasn't reduced or stopped the epidermic of depression and suicide! If material riches, wealth and financial success can fill the vacuum within man, then there wouldn't be a reason for depression among the rich or increasing cases of suicide. The United States of America is not left out of this ugly situation. It is the richest and most prosperous and powerful nation on Earth, yet it is still struggling with the 'national epidemic' of gun control, as referred to by President Biden.

We hear of touching and regretful incidences where

people take guns into public places and start shooting and killing people with reckless abandon, without any sense of regards for human lives! There is a yearning and deep craving within every man to be happy and fulfilled; success and prosperity can secure you anything you want in life, but only by answering the call of Destiny can you become intrinsically satisfied and fulfilled.

challenges and problems of man are a wake-up call for someone's potentials, gifts and talents

The persistence of problems in society is evidence that someone has not really answered the call of Destiny because all challenges and problems of man are a wake-up call for someone's potentials, gifts and talents. Everyone on Earth was designed to solve one particular problem or the other, so as to make the world a safer and better place. Therefore, the continuous persistence of unsolved problems reveal the truth that someone hasn't accepted the responsibility of answering the call of Destiny; the unsolved problems are not impossible cases, as my model clearly explained in the previous chapter, but lack of capacity and competence cases. When we all arise from our beds of slumber and laziness to accept the responsibility of answering the call of Destiny, we will realise that nothing is impossible on Earth.

Genesis 11:4-6,
And they said, Go to, let us build us a city and a tower, whose top may reach unto heaven: and let us make us a name, lest we be scattered abroad upon the face of the whole earth.
And the LORD came down to see the city and the tower, which the children had built.
And the LORD said, behold, the people is one, and they have all one language; and this they begin to do: and nothing will be restrained from them, which they have imagined to do.

There is nothing anyone will imagine that will be impossible to achieve, because nothing is impossible. Whatever the human mind can conceive, it can be achieved. Everyone was created to solve a problem, so the present and persistent continuity of life's problems is an indication that someone who was created to solve that problem is still sleeping, and that he has his giant still sleeping within and needs to be awakened. It's time for everyone to begin to answer the call of destiny in his life, because the world we live in is in darkness and in a very big mess. There has never been a greater time in history when great leaders, thinkers and solution providers are needed than in the present times. We are in times of uncertainty and peril, the like of which has never been seen before. This is the time for people to awaken the sleeping giant within them in order to proffer solutions to these multitudes of problems that have befallen our generation.

Whatever the human mind can conceive, it can be achieved.

Crisis is a wake-up call for our potentials; problems and difficulties of life are nothing but alarms of destiny to stir up the sleeping giants that have been lying dormant within us. There has never been such an urgency for leaders to rise in any generation than the one we are in, because of the numerous problems that have befallen our generation. Nothing is impossible; none of these problems facing us now are impossible to be solved. It just means the men of capacity and competence must rise, men must discover themselves and answer the call of destiny in order to proffer solutions to this problem threatening the existence of mankind.

Everyone has a star within him; everyone has a giant within him; and everyone has something great to offer to his or her generation. Until the person decides to accept the call of destiny, the person might never rise from obscurity into greatness to the height that God has prepared for everyone. It is time to wake up from our slumber and awaken the sleeping giant within and answer the call of destiny, and only by doing this shall we rise to greatness without end. This is the only way to reach fulfilment and satisfaction.

BELIEVE IN YOUR DESTINY

The first step to rising from the dust of laziness and the shackles and fetters of mediocrity to answer the call of destiny is to believe in yourself and in the boundless possibilities of your destiny; you really have to first believe that there is a destiny that God prepared for you, before your conception and birth, into this beautiful world. Everyone's birth in this world is proof that he or she was created or designed to solve a particular problem; if you were not needed on Earth, there wouldn't have been any need for your birth, as no manufacturer designs and produces any product without a particular function and need. And don't expect God to be the victim of such carelessness and absolute waste of time in creating anyone without a purpose to fulfil here on Earth. This is why you have to believe in the authenticity and greatness of the destiny that lies ahead of you and within you.

There is a glory of God that will be revealed in you and through you, and that can only come about when you decide to rise up and answer this call of destiny in order to preserve the next generation from decadence. If you do nothing to answer the clarion call of destiny, the next generation will suffer, because you are meant to fill a gap that should not be passed on to the next generation. The life we live in is like a relay race, where members of a team take turns in order to complete parts of a race consisting of a number of stages. Each stage is run by a different member of the team, whereby the runner completing a stage passes the baton to the awaiting runner ahead, who runs another stage and also passes the baton to another team member until the race is finished. One team member has to run from one point to another and hands over the baton to the next person ahead, who continues until the race is finished. But when there is an interruption along the line, such that a particular runner with the baton breaks down or gives up, or for whatever reason didn't pass on the baton to the next runner by not completing his own stage or leg, there will be a huge challenge and delay because the next person is left with a greater and deeper burden to cover up the laps created by the previous runner. He will be forced to draw back to collect the baton and that will cost the team dearly.

This is how it happens in normal life; we live on Earth by stages or generations, where the present generation will have to pass the baton of development, success, discoveries, progress and advancement to the next generation. Even in families this is apparent. The parents run their race by living their lives and passing on the baton to the next generation, which is the children, and the children live their lives and pass the baton to the next generation, and so it continues. That is how family names are preserved for posterity or from extinction.

In the eastern part of Nigeria, male child bearing is the most critical factor that keeps the family together. A man can go to any length, including taking as many wives as possible just to give birth to a male child, who they believe will be the one to bear his name and preserve the family from extinction. It doesn't matter how many female children the man has if his wife doesn't give birth to a son; he will go to any length to have a son. But the question is, what kind of baton are you passing onto your children, to your family, to your employees and to the next generation after you? Some pass the right values to their children, who go on to excel in life, while others pass on the wrong values, which eventually destroy the future of their generation.

Recently, I was interviewing a couple at my place of internship who have been married for more than two decades and are still living together in peace, love and unity. However, their daughter, who had recently married, had divorced just less than three years into her marriage and returned back to this couple's home with her child. It got me worrying and, out of curiosity, I asked the couple, 'What is the secret that has kept you people together in marriage for decades, while your daughter who has been married for less than three years has divorced? What is the secret? What do you people know that we, the younger generation, need to know?' I was stunned at the response I got from them! They said that, in their generation, they listened to their parents, there was fear of the Lord, their parents used to scold them, punish and spank them when they misbehaved; teachers used to whip them at school when they misbehaved, and they used to go to church. But they said that everything has changed now, that it's no longer the same now, that parents are the ones who are afraid of their children. The younger generation don't go to church anymore, teachers don't have the right to whip students at school, nor even scold them, and the children of the present generation are no longer under the guidance and discipline of their parents.

Then, inadvertently, I asked a question that I 'probably shouldn't have asked'! Impulsively and instinctively, I asked, 'Would I be wrong to say that you parents have failed, since you were not able to pass the same values and moral upbringing to your children that your own parents passed down to you?' They were startled and taken aback. I observed the looks of anger and sadness on their faces; they withdrew backward and, because there were other people listening, in order to save their faces, they responded, 'Well, you are not really right, it's the modernisation and freedom of everything in this country that has caused it, not necessarily parental failure to instil the right discipline into the children.'

The kind of foundation you lay for your children will determine the outcome of the next generation. There is such a large generation gap in our present generation; the older generation owes the younger generation so much information they need to excel and triumph and, if they refuse to tell the younger generation the truth about life, there will be crises, chaos and so much complexities and burdens for them. In order not to create a deeper problem, burden and pressure for the next generation, then you must rise and accept that there is a destiny that only you can fulfil, and if you don't rise to accept and answer this clarion call to fulfil your destiny, future generations will perish and struggle for survival.

There are lives and destinies that are connected to you; generations ahead of you are also connected to your rising to answer the call of destiny, and if you don't rise up to the occasion, they will struggle to achieve balance and stability in their times. There are things yet to be discovered, inventions waiting to be made, life-transforming books to be written, inspiring songs to be sung, businesses to be established and so many problems to be solved in these present times. If no one rises to the demands and challenges of our times, then the burden will be greater on the generations to come because we have refused to carry out our responsibilities and fulfil our parts of the task which behoves us to do.

It is important to understand that everyone has a place on Earth, everyone has a function to fulfil and everyone has an assignment to execute. However, if that thing is not done properly, then a gap will be created, and those gaps will put a burden and pressure on the future generations and, consequently, putting more responsibilities than are required on the next generation so as to cover up those gaps and achieve balance and stability.

For instance, someone from a very poor background, deprived of many of the good things of life and a good upbringing, will work harder to excel and become great as much as another person who was privileged to be born into a rich home with the right moral upbringing, virtues and access to all the good things of life. The reason being that the parents did their due diligence, paid their own price and played their own parts, in that they didn't transfer their struggles, poverty and limitations to their children or the next generation. Research and statistics have proven that children who were abused early in life tend to be associated with crimes later in life. One such publication is:

Lorraine E. Cuadra, Anna E. Jaffe, Renu Thomas, David DiLillo, Child maltreatment and adult criminal behavior: Does criminal thinking explain the association?,
Child Abuse & Neglect, (2014)
https://doi.org/10.1016/j.chiabu.2014.02.005.
(https://www.sciencedirect.com/science/article/pii/S0145213414000441)

The foundation of a child's upbringing matters so much in the matters of fulfilment of destiny. But it doesn't matter whether you were abused or not, if you have read through this book to this chapter, you would have been equipped with the secrets to turning every situation around. A child who comes from a wealthy home has already had a great foundation laid by the parents, because the parents played their own parts in accepting responsibility for destiny and greatness, thereby making the future better and brighter for their children and the next generation. I will give two clear examples. First, being born into the British Royal family gives you access to all the privileges that life has to offer, yet a person can still decide to be irresponsible. Another family I respect is that of Dr. David O. Oyedepo, the founder of Living Faith Church, born into a poor family. He decided to answer the call of destiny and became prosperous and wealthy. His first son, Pastor David O. Oyedepo Jr, took advantage of the great foundation his father had laid and he is now the presiding Pastor of the 50,000-seater church auditorium – which was once the largest church auditorium in the world – while still in his early thirties, a very young age.

But those parents who didn't accept responsibility for success and greatness and answer the call of destiny end up transferring greater responsibilities, burdens and great pressures to their children and the generations ahead. Consequently, if they don't develop the required competence and capacity to solve the problems that their parents were

DESTINY IS CALLING

supposed to have solved, it will create a very big gap and make it appear to be an impossible case. Like I said, there is no impossibility anywhere! Impossibility is just a term that is used to refer to unsolved problems and these are as a result of a lack of adequate capacity and competence to solve the problems. Anybody who refuses to accept responsibility for success and greatness in order to fulfil their destiny is only creating an imbalance in the system and transferring greater responsibility than is necessary to the generations unborn; and, when the next generation comes along, they will be faced with greater responsibilities and challenges because the previous generations refused to play their own parts by accepting responsibility with diligence and commitment.

This is how the next generation can be secured. The only way we can seek to secure the future of the next generation is by taking responsibility for ourselves, responsibility to solve the problems that are before us and not to shift them to the next generation to suffer, because everyone is designed to solve a particular problem, and also by developing a high level of competence and capacity. If the level of capacity and competence developed is insufficient to solve the bigger problems that were pushed ahead by the previous generation, then it will look like a case of impossibility; however, that was the problem that should have been solved, but there were no men or women willing to accept the call of destiny.

It's time for everyone to accept this call, to answer the call of destiny for the sake of the next generation. If you believe in your significance to the world, then you will rise up to take responsibility and answer the call of destiny. It's abnormal as a responsible person not to feel the problems of people. Don't you see the countless millions of lives in poverty and in pain? It is important to have an awareness in you of the urgency to rise up, to proffer a solution to the darkness and problems that have befallen creation; the world is facing many challenges and this is a time for you to believe in your own significance to the world and rise up to offer to the world the blessing within you. There is greatness within you; there is something of great value that the world has not seen that is still within you; but not until you decide to answer the call of destiny will it find expression in the world, and that is where your true happiness, joy, satisfaction and fulfilment will come from.

YOU CAN OVERTURN ANY SITUATION

The only way to prove people wrong in your life is to rise up and answer the call of destiny. I understand that there are people who wish failure on others and expect people to fail; however, the only way you can prove people's negative expectation of you is to rise up and accept your responsibility to fulfil the great destiny that lies inside of you and ahead of you. You can overcome people's evil and negative imagination and expectation of you and prove them wrong by making them know that you are not a failure. It is certain that many people will have their own opinion and conclusion of you, many will call you different names, some will say nothing good can ever come out of you and that is the reason they treated you badly, but you know what? You are not going to let them win; you are not going to prove them right; you are not going to make them feel that they have won. That is why you have to rise up and give your destiny the fight of your life by accepting responsibility for its actualisation.

I advise you not to be discouraged and depressed because of people's negative opinions and conclusions about you; rather, let that be the reason why you will rise up to the challenge and demand your destiny. Destiny is a great responsibility and its path is paved with challenges and obstacles because of its inestimable value, and that is where your beauty and glory will emanate from, but the challenges are not insurmountable.

DESTINY HAS DEMANDS
'Every man is responsible for his own destiny.'
– Liu Kan

As you believe in the possibilities of your destiny and believe in yourself, you have to also understand that destiny has enormous demands and sacrifices to be made in order to achieve it. Destiny is not achieved on a bed of roses and it's never achieved by sleeping all day; effort and serious commitments must be made to follow due diligence in order to fulfil your destiny. I strongly believe this is one of the reasons why many people decide to lead an ordinary life because they are not willing and ready to be committed to the demands of destiny. Every man of outstanding impact and greatness in life is a man of great sacrifice and commitment because, without it, no one can fulfil a glorious destiny.

The demands of destiny will require you to keep late nights, to go the extra mile, to invest in yourself consistently, to keep improving yourself, to keep reinventing yourself, to keep stretching yourself beyond your present limits, and every other necessary commitment to be competent and to develop the capacity required to fulfil destiny. In light of this, Dr. Mike Murdock said, 'Your assignment will require your total focus, seasons of intensified prayer and fasting, and seasons of prayerful isolation.' Fulfilment of destiny requires your preparation and investment in yourself in order to develop the competences and capacity required to fulfil it, so never assume that greatness and success just happens.

Anything great and worthwhile must be adequately prepared for because destiny doesn't just happen to people, greatness doesn't just happen to people, impact and influence don't just happen to people, progress and prosperity don't just happen to people. It is worked out; it is carefully planned and prepared for, and that is the true path and the only way it can be fulfilled.

FIGHTING FOR YOUR DESTINY

'Destiny is usually just around the corner. Like a thief, a hooker, or a lottery vendor: its three most common personifications. But what destiny does not do is home visits. You have to go for it.' – Carlos Ruiz Zafón

Another important thing to understand is that there will always be obstacles and limitations in your path to the fulfilment of your glorious destiny and that is why you must put up the 'fight of destiny'. You must be willing to fight for it and to go all out for it because, without fighting for it, you can never win, neither can you fulfil destiny. You are going to experience moments of isolation, confrontations, oppositions, challenges and trials that will be put in your way, but you must not give up; you must not be discouraged, nor distracted. In the words of Dr. Mike Murdock, 'Crisis is a normal event on the road to your assignment.'

You will have to understand that the challenges and oppositions don't come to destroy you, but they come to prove you; they come to test you and they come to challenge your readiness, willingness and resolve to fulfil destiny, because it is in the moment of trials and temptations that the strength and stamina required to fulfil destiny are developed. It is pertinent to understand that anything worthwhile is worth fighting for; only great things of value are contested for. People contest for political offices such as presidency, governorship and other important political offices because of the values and prestige they hold. You will never see a country where the office of the presidency will be run by just one candidate unopposed, because everything of value is greatly desired and contested for! In the midst of the numerous contestants or candidates for a particular trophy, you don't give up.

No ever goes into any competition in any field, sports or other areas, to contest for the second position; only the first position is contested for. The trophy is not without a fierce contest! So, you don't run away from challenges and obstacles, never run away from oppositions and confrontations or negative situations in life; they come to bring out the best in you, they come to make you strong, not to break you; they come to equip you in order to fulfil destiny, and that is why you must be ready to fight for it against all odds. For more on this, I encourage you to look for my book *Against All Odds*. Don't think it's going to come easy, don't think it's going to just drop on you, don't think your enemies are just going to let you go and fulfil destiny without a fight. Little wonder that Mike Murdock said, 'The completion of your assignment is your enemy's greatest fear.'

I can assure you that you will face and experience a lot of trials, challenges and moments that will make you feel like giving up. But it is times like that when you must remember that it is a fight you must complete, it is a fight you must not transfer to your next generation, it is a fight you must not leave to your children to fight. Don't think of transferring your fights and battles to your next generation; you have to rise up and fight it now, so that the destinies of your children unborn and generations ahead can be secured and preserved from decadence and destruction.

DESTINY REQUIRES PREPARATION

It is also very important to understand that every great destiny requires a great preparation to fulfil it; it's not enough to believe in your destiny and in yourself, but you must also prepare for the destiny you desire to fulfil. The responsibility and burden of destiny is the reason for which you must be prepared for it; destiny fulfilment requires adequate time for preparation, and it is in the season of your preparation that competence and capacity are developed.

In support of this truth, Dr. Mike Murdock said, 'Your assignment will require seasons of preparation.' And, according to Dr. David O. Oyedepo, 'No one ever arrives at a future he cannot see, neither does anyone arrive at a future he is not prepared for. No giant ever emerged in any field without adequate preparation for their pursuit.'

The consciousness of destiny will make you lead a meticulous, principled and separated lifestyle; it is the consciousness of destiny that will define the kind of decisions you will make because, eventually, the height anyone will ever attain in life will be dependent upon the quality of the decisions he or she makes. It is your destiny-consciousness that virtually controls everything that you will choose to do, and sometimes the consciousness of destiny will even determine or control what you eat, what you wear, where you go, your associations, the kind of jobs that you do and, of course, the choice of a life partner. This is the most important and critical area of our lives, where destiny-consciousness decisions affect us mostly, because the choice for your life partner can determine the outcome of the rest of your life.

In my own opinion, don't choose a life partner until you have discovered your destiny, and know what you're going to do to fulfil your destiny in order to avoid some unnecessary crises later in life. Destiny has demands and preparation in order to fulfil it and that is why the choice of a life partner is the most critical aspect in decision-making towards the fulfilment of destiny. You can't marry someone who does not believe in your destiny, or who does not have faith and conviction in your pursuits for life. Therefore, destiny-decisions affect every aspect of your life, but especially the decision of whom you wish to spend the rest of your life with.

DESTINY PAYS BACK
'I am comfortable at the height where destiny has put me.'
– Pranab Mukherjee

The driving force behind my commitment to fulfil destiny is the consciousness that destiny pays back. The most valuable and profitable investment is investment in your destiny because it will pay you beyond your imagination and what no other company shares or bonds can ever pay. Whatever

DESTINY IS CALLING

sacrifices and investment you make into your destiny, it will never be a loss; destiny always ensures that nothing ever invested into it, or sacrificed for it, ever goes unrewarded. Every effort you put into your destiny to see its fulfilment will, in return, pay you back enormously. No employer can ever pay you half of what destiny can pay if you decide to labour for your destiny.

No one in life will be poor if everyone decides to labour for their destiny

No one in life will be poor if everyone decides to labour for their destiny there would be no poverty in our world if everyone made it a conscious effort to labour and sacrifice for their destinies. Your destiny is crying out for attention; just invest everything you have into it and it will return that investment back to you in a multiplied and glorified form. It's time to listen to the cry of destiny and attend to it, because that is the path of the making of every great man and woman on planet Earth. Destiny is the fairest and best employer and pay master; there is no other job that can pay you the way destiny can; there is no employer that can pay you half of what destiny will pay you; there is no organisation on the face of the Earth that can pay you ten percent of what destiny can pay you. When destiny pays you, it settles you for life; it doesn't just pay financially or materially, it pays one in all aspects of life. Above all, it brings you joy, satisfaction, fulfilment and greatness.

The greatness that everyone desires lies in the hands of destiny; all the good things of life and the great future that everyone desires can be found in destiny. Destiny has everything you are looking for and destiny is willing and ready to pay you back, but only if you are ready to pay the price to accept the responsibility, make the sacrifices and commitment and fight for its actualisation.

The beginning might be rough, there might be hardship and obstacles in your way that threaten you and make you want to give up on destiny, but never give up in the pursuit of greatness, never give up on destiny. You must keep the hope of your destiny alive; you must believe in destiny, you must be convinced about the reality and validity of the greatness of your destiny. Above all, you must be committed to the actualisation of your destiny.

Afterwards, your investment in your destiny will pay off; destiny will, in turn, begin to pay you back in numerous ways that you could never have imagined. Destiny will take you to great heights that you never saw, destiny will bring you into greatness that you never imagined, destiny will give you connections that you never bargained for, destiny will bring you boundless opportunities no one could have offered you in life, destiny will give you wealth and riches that you could never have worked for. Destiny will give you more peace, joy, fulfilment and satisfaction than anything on Earth can bring. Destiny is worth fighting for and this why I charge and challenge you to accept the responsibility and answer the clarion call of destiny in your life.

You may succeed if nobody believes in you, but you will never succeed if you don't believe in yourself.
—John C. Maxwell

CHAPTER SEVEN
IF YOU MUST SUCCEED, BELIEVE IN YOURSELF

'You may succeed if nobody believes in you, but you will never succeed if you don't believe in yourself.'
—John C. Maxwell

I feel highly motivated writing about this chapter 'believe in yourself', because the totality of my life story can be summed up in those three words 'believe in yourself' and. I have had encounters with some people whose lives were dramatically changed by the power of self-belief. A perfect example of the power of believing in one's self is that of a big brother and friend, whom I had the privilege of meeting personally a couple of years ago. His life story is one that everyone should hear and be inspired by. I am so happy writing about it because, to a very great extent, his life has inspired me to keep fighting for what I believed in; he literally boosted my self-belief and I would be proud to say that he is the person that has practically demonstrated the principle of self-belief. He is a perfect case study of what it means to believe in yourself. I thought I actually believed in myself until I met him, but then I knew I was still far from believing in myself and I learnt the principle of self-belief from him.

His name is Chijioke Okonkwo, a man from the Eastern part of Nigeria. He is married with three lovely children, a successful businessman, philanthropist, and an entrepreneur. I heard him share his story of how he became a multimillionaire and eventually a multibillionaire. He is from a humble background and comes from a family and clan where it was difficult, or nearly impossible, for a young man to succeed, let alone erect a structure for a house!

If you must succeed, you must believe in yourself

But he proved that nothing is impossible if you are willing and committed to achieving greatness in life. He is a man that has always believed in greatness, even when there was nothing that spelled or gave a hint of greatness around him, nor his background. His background was enough to prove to him that greatness was an impossibility as there was no one that knew what success or greatness was, and so he decided to change the narratives of his background, family and the entire community he comes from.

He once worked for a private firm but was never satisfied as there was something inside of him that always told him, 'Guy, you are more than this, there's something bigger than this for you, you can be greater than this. If others can make it big, then I can too. If there is anyone in this life who is successful, then I too can be successful.' So he decided to quit his job to pursue greatness, to discover the source and become a manufacturer of wealth instead of being just a retailer.

Chijioke Okonkwo's first attempt was when he saw an opportunity where one of the top-ranking banks in Nigeria advertised for bidders to bid for a contract worth 1 billion naira and he saw it as an opportunity to apply. For those in the construction industry, you will understand the rigorous processes and qualifications needed to win a bid to construct complex buildings. Some of the compulsory requirements will be to show your expertise in construction and track records of your efficiency in successfully completing complex projects and, of course, a clientele list.

But, most critically, you also need to have the financial capability to execute such projects as you will be given a little percentage as mobilisation fee, and you will be required to finance the project as proof of your financial capability and expertise.

To spare you the long story, Chijioke didn't have any of these criteria. Nevertheless, he went to bid for the contract. The tough thing about it was that major multinationals in the construction industry and other top-ranking men in the political corridors who owned construction firms applied and would use their powers and connection to influence it, especially those who knew the managing director of the bank. So, the odds were against him. He had no sensible and justifiable reason to bid for the contract because he didn't have the expertise, he had never worked on such contracts before, even though he trained as a Civil Engineer. But self-confidence and belief in one's self don't consider the environmental or external factors; they control the external from within. Those who believe in themselves live from inside-out, they are not controlled by people or the external world; rather, they control from within them, or internally, what goes on around them.

As Theodore Roosevelt once said, 'Believe you can and you're halfway there.' This shows how much of an advantage one will have if they believe in themselves.

So, Chijioke submitted his proposal, as an individual contractor. Note that in such major contracts, you mostly bid as a corporate entity, but in his case he decided to bid as an individual. Eventually, they were invited for interview and when it was his turn, the manager asked him, 'Let me see your bank statement, your financial capacity!' When Chijioke presented it, the manager laughed at him said, 'What gave you the guts to even think of applying for this contract? You don't have any equipment for this contract, neither do you have the financial capacity even to rent one, so why did you even think of bidding for this contract?' You know, it's normal for people not to believe in you and you will definitely meet a lot of people who don't believe in you, but if you must succeed in this life, you must believe in yourself. Chijioke responded, 'I can do it better than anyone else. Besides, if I run away, you people can hold

> *People may not believe in you and it's normal with life; but if you must be successful, you must believe in yourself.*

me accountable and prosecute me, but if any of those top politicians and organisations run away with your money, you can't do anything to them because of their powers and position. So, if you really want to execute your contract successfully, better award it to someone you can trust and hold accountable.'

You may succeed if nobody believes in you, but you will never succeed if you don't believe in yourself. John C. Maxwell

They were startled and stunned by his confidence and composure. Eventually, he was awarded the contract. But not having the expertise, the capacity and financial capability, he sold the contract to a third party for 900 million naira and monitored the execution till it was successfully completed. He became 900 million naira richer in one day, not for inventing anything but just in believing in himself; and, as a wise man, he has multiplied that money and he is a multibillionaire today, helping and investing in young people. I have never seen an individual that commits to the development of young people in Nigeria and probably in the world like him.

But this was a young man who decided to get married even when he had nothing; and, in order to survive, he had to live separately from his wife for a couple of years. He moved into his friend's house while his wife had a small place to put up with. This he did so he could ease the pressures of life and make both ends meet. A young visionary man, who wouldn't let his poor background make him feel inferior, nor allow another to treat him with disdain and disrespect because of his unpleasant and unpalatable circumstances. His friend began to treat him wrongly and disdainfully, without any form of respect simply because he paid the bills and provided for his feeding, but Chijioke Okonkwo wouldn't accept such treatment, nor allow his self-esteem to be jeopardised by his friend due to his unpleasant circumstances. He is a man of strong convictions in himself and his potentials to excel in life. Instead of allowing his friend to make him look inferior and damage his self-esteem and confidence, he decided to vacate his friend's house and join his wife. The good ending of the story is that even his friend is nowhere close to him in success and achievement. A young man that has sponsored hundreds of young people on full scholarships abroad is not a small man! I wish the world had 'two of his type'. The world would have become a better place and many poor people would have been lifted out of poverty!

MY PERSONAL EXPERIENCE WITH HIM

Chijioke Okonkwo walked into my life at the most crucial point of my life, when I needed help the most. I was seeking direction in my life and hoping to excel and achieve my dreams one day. First, when I started my industrial cleaning firm in Nigeria, he pushed and inspired me to start it and he gave me the first and biggest contract I ever had. When things became difficult and I got stuck in the wake of Covid-19, his words of inspirations were my anchor. He always told me these words, 'There is no space anywhere in life; you have to create your own space.' He told me these words when I was almost giving up because of the struggles I was experiencing. I had it very rough then and almost thought that I had come to the end of the road. I would complain about the difficulties and hardships, more especially the disappointments I had from people, and was about to blame people and the government for the difficult predicaments I was in. But each time, he would reach out to me and ask, 'Guy, what's up? What is happening?' After explaining to him, he would say to me, countless number of times, 'Keep pushing, you are nearer to success than you can imagine.'

There is no space anywhere in life; you have to create your own space.

Chijioke Okonkwo

Believe in Yourself

His words most times were 'keep pushing', 'keep pushing' and 'keep pushing' and sincerely, those words became the anchor of my soul and I ran with those words. I kept pushing and, today, I have made more success and progress in a short while (less than three years) that I have known him than I have made in over 30 years of my life, and I am still pushing and will keep pushing till I get to the zenith of my potentials and become the best I can possibly become in my lifetime. The most interesting part of the story is that he became the sponsor of my master's degree programme in the UK. He believed in me and took financial responsibility for the financial costs and I am ever grateful to him for giving me such a lifetime opportunity to pursue my dreams. He went from poverty to prosperity, and today he is responsible for the success of countless numbers of young people in Nigeria. He has sponsored so many young people to further their studies in different parts of the world though his academic scholarship programme, and empowered many others in starting businesses and living meaningfully. His businesses have grown to become global empires and conglomerates by thinking and dreaming big, and also believing in himself.

Keep pushing, you are closer to success than you can ever imagine.

Chijioke Okonkwo

I wish everyone could understand the power of this words: keep pushing, you are closer to success than you can ever imagine. Many people have given up in life, not knowing how close they were to success before they gave up. If everyone would learn to keep pushing and never give up in the face of overwhelming odds, there

So many people fail, not because they don't have the right idea or are doing the wrong things, but because they gave up too soon before their success

would be less mediocre and failures in life. So many people fail, not because they don't have the right idea or are doing the wrong things, but because they gave up too soon before their success – their success-belief drive wasn't sufficient enough to take them to the success-belief threshold.

Those who believe in themselves are those who keep pushing in the midst of challenges and contradictory evidences. The first key of success is believing in yourself that you can do it; without this, you will easily give up when obstacles show up and they will certainly show up because difficulties and trials are part of the success process. Only those who believe in themselves can keep pushing beyond the limitations of life until they achieve the victory they seek.

YOU NEED SOMEONE TO BELIEVE IN YOU
'Every one of us needs someone to believe in us long enough for us to develop the inner strength to believe in ourselves... Find yourself a Mentor!'
—**Dov Baron**

By studying the lives of successful people, I have found that, at one point or the other in their lives, they had someone who gave them an opportunity to succeed, an opportunity to prove themselves. We all need someone to believe in us, to give us an opportunity, because if no one believes in you they won't stake their chances on you Even for a man to marry a lady, she needs to believe in him first and be convinced in him to give him the chance. One of my senior friends, Orji Obioma Reuben, on celebrating his wife's birthday posted on Facebook, 'My greatest and most brilliant achievement in life was my ability to convince my wife to marry me'. Until people believe in you, they might never give you a chance or opportunity in life, and life is all about the opportunities one gets and eventually maximises, because the

'The greatness of one's life lies in the number of opportunities they took advantage of.'

Believe in Yourself

The first key of success is believing in yourself that you can do it; without this, you will easily give up when obstacles show up

greatness of one's life can't be separated from the opportunities you get in life.

Everyone whoever succeeded in life was given an opportunity at one point or other to prove themselves and to prove their capability to succeed, because in this life you can never really succeed without the input of people in your life. If people don't give you the opportunity needed to excel, you might never succeed in life and no one will ever know what you are made of.

Most great men in life are great because they had an opportunity to manifest their potentials, and someone created the right environment for them to excel. One person or the other believed in them and that was why they were able to succeed. For instance, in football, no matter the talents and skills you have, if no team ever gives you an opportunity to play for them you might die unknown an unheard of. Actually, great athletes are people that had the opportunity to display their skills; if no club ever gives you an opportunity, you will never ever excel. It doesn't matter the skills and talents a player has, if he is always on the bench or never admitted by any club, such a person will never see the light of day and the world will never hear of him.

There are many unheard of and unknown potential heroes who are still in their bedrooms and villages because no one gave them an opportunity to prove themselves. There are still potentially greater players than Cristiano Ronaldo and Lionel Messi who are still confined at the backside of the mountain simply because no one believed in them enough to give them an opportunity, or they never had an opportunity to display their talents. There are countless numbers of unsung heroes and heroines whom the world never knew because they didn't get an opportunity to prove their worth, unread

> *We all need someone to believe in us, to give us an opportunity, because if no one believes in you they won't stake their chances on you*

and unknown books that would have become bestselling books if a publisher believed in them enough to get the books published, and unheard songs that would have produced world-class artistes if they had an opportunity to releaser the songs.

The Bible makes it clear that people can lack the opportunity to display or show their attitude, talents or do what they intend to do. Someone might have the good desire to do something or a great idea for a business or something but never get the opportunity to execute it.

But I rejoiced in the Lord greatly, that now at the last your care of me hath flourished again: wherein ye were also careful, but ye LACKED OPPORTUNITY.
Philippians 4:10

I believe the world has not yet seen the best of talented and gifted men. Every day in the headline news we hear of staggering accomplishments of people that the world never thought was possible a few decades and centuries past. I still believe if we take a walk to the cemetery and take statistics, we would find greater players than the world has ever known in there, because they died with their potentials unknown as they didn't have the opportunity that others had. We would find greater scientists and inventors than what the world knows today, we would find great leaders that would have reshaped our world today but didn't have the opportunity to serve the world with their gifts.

> *'Your level of success in life is not different from the opportunities you maximised.'*

If we went to the cemetery to check, we would still find all kinds of strange and dynamic potentials that would have been greater than what the world knows today as greatness,

Believe in Yourself

but they didn't have anyone to give them the opportunity to shine their lights. It is obvious that people's level of success in life is no different from the opportunities they maximised.

Everyone needs someone to give them an opportunity to excel. My big brother Chijioke Okonkwo was able to make that huge amount of money simply because that bank believed in him and gave him the opportunity to execute the contract. However, he didn't excel simply because the bank gave him an opportunity to execute the contract, but because he actually took advantage of it and made the most of it. That is why I believe that having opportunities is good, but making the most of them is what counts. The Bible says,

As we have opportunity therefore, let us do good unto all men, especially unto them who are of the household of faith.
Galatians 6.

'Having opportunities is good, but making the most of them is what counts.'

I have observed that when we trust and have faith in ourselves, we are only presented with an opportunity to prove ourselves. It's not faith in ourselves and in God that what gets the job done. No! When we believe in ourselves and in our capabilities, God in one way or the other presents to us opportunities so we can take advantage of them and prove what stuff we are made of. Greatness is nothing but the opportunities we all took advantages of.

Life is all about taking advantage of opportunities. Every success a person makes is traceable to the opportunities they took advantage of. Your success can never be greater than the opportunities you took advantage of. The things we call risks are opportunities life presents

'God doesn't send us money from heaven, He only gives people opportunities to make money.'

IF YOU MUST SUCCEED, BELIEVE IN YOURSELF

'The things we call risks are opportunities in disguise.'

to everyone to take advantage of and excel. However, having opportunity is not what makes one successful, but their ability to turn the opportunities into success, being able to take the opportunity and make the most of it.

There are stories of people who are poor and unsuccessful in life not because they were born poor, but because they never took advantage of the opportunities life gave to them. I have seen countless number of people waste the opportunities that life gave to them; there are people who had greater opportunities than others, yet couldn't make anything out of it. While growing up, I had friends whose parents were rich and gave them all the luxuries of life and sent them to good schools, but eventually they ended up very badly because they couldn't take advantage of the opportunities life gave to them. Being from a wealthy background is not what makes people successful and great; rather, it is the opportunity life gave to such people to become successful.

It is certain we don't all have equal opportunities in life, but eventually every one of us will be judged by the opportunities life gave to us. Looking back, I would observe that there were people I knew who had fewer opportunities compared to others while growing up; but, years later, those who had little or no opportunities had become more successful and greater than those folks who had more opportunities.

'One's life can't be greater than the number of opportunities they maximised.'

I have a cousin by the name of Talent Sidi who has Scottish citizenship, is married and doing well in the UK. I grew up with him and he was the least expected to be successful in life. He had older brothers who had far better opportunities than him; he didn't really do well, but his eldest sister (Khun Sidi) gave him just one opportunity to study for his Master's degree in the UK. When he got to the airport

> *'One opportunity maximised is better than missed or unutilized multiple opportunities.'*

in the UK and called her to inform her he had arrived, she said to him, 'Talent, you have just one stone in your sling, shoot and make sure you don't misfire because that is all you have.' Today, as he shared with me personally, he sends money to those who had greater opportunities than him back then.

There are many people who had plenty of opportunities but never used them well, while there are others who had just one and they maximised that opportunity and made the most of it, and are better off than those who had them aplenty.

So, it's not about having multiple opportunities, but being able to make the most of them. Like someone rightly said, nothing is more expensive than a missed opportunity. ***The greatness of one's life lies in the number of opportunities they took advantage of.***

THESE WORDS OF INSPIRATION WILL INSPIRE YOU

- *One's life can't be greater than the number of opportunities they maximised.*
- *Your level of success in life is no different from the opportunities you maximised.*
- *Life is a stream of opportunities and only those who are prepared take advantage of them.*
- *We are all surrounded by opportunities every day, only those who are wise can see them.*
- *The things we call risks are opportunities in disguise.*
- *God doesn't send us money from heaven, He only gives people opportunities to make money.*
- *Having opportunities is good, but making the most of them is what counts.*

YOU NEED TO BELIEVE IN PEOPLE

To succeed in life, you can't do it all alone. You can't succeed in life by being alone or working alone, because God didn't design life to be lived in isolation. One of the causes of depression is isolation; there is no successful or great man on Earth who didn't have at least someone who believed in them and inspired them to push, push harder and to keep pushing in life. There will always be a point where you need the support of people to get to the next level of progress in life. We all need to believe in other people for two primary reasons: firstly, to give people the opportunity to prove themselves and, secondly, to enable us to build the right team to fulfil our assignment and achieve our goals in life.

In order to build something great, you will need concerted efforts and an effective team to do that, and you can never build a formidable team if you don't believe in people. To be able to harness the best out of people and make them give you their best, you must believe in them, even when they don't or can't believe in themselves. In the words of Dov Baron, 'Every one of us needs someone to believe in us long enough for us to develop the inner strength to believe in ourselves... Find yourself a Mentor!'

Most times, great leaders will first believe in their followers and team members before the followers will develop self-confidence in themselves and begin to excel. There are times you really have to tell someone, 'You have all it takes to succeed, I believe in you, if you can just give it a little more push, you will excel.' These are inspiring words of leaders to their followers who are still lambs, but who can be turned into lions. It takes a good leader to turn the lambs among their followers into lions, cowards into a formidable army, and weaklings into warriors and valiant men; and all these can only be achieved if the leader believes in the people he is called upon to lead.

'Every one of us needs someone to believe in us long

enough for us to develop the inner strength to believe in ourselves... Find yourself a Mentor!'
—**Dov Baron**

There are many 'crude oil-like' followers, or people who are like potential motor gasoline, aviation gasoline, fuel, lubricants, paraffin, wax, petroleum coke, Hydrocarbon gas liquids, kerosene, etc. You need to believe in them before you can harness the great potentials within them in order to achieve your purpose. The most indispensable prolific people today were once novices, crude and raw, but were turned into the great assets they are now for their organisations or leaders because someone saw a potential greatness and value in them, and also believed in them enough to commit to their growth and development. If you see people being very loyal to their bosses to the extent of death, or that they respect someone highly to the point where they can't betray or disappoint them, even if it costs them their lives, check it closely. You will find that such people believed in them when no one else could, when there was nothing that resembled greatness in them, but transformed them into the greatness they now are. So, they remain eternally loyal and committed to following their bosses or leaders.

When you read about how Peter and all the Apostles laid down their lives for Jesus and died to defend their faith in Him, you will realise that Peter was an ordinary fisherman who was giving up on life and his fishing career when Jesus met him and turned his life around. An uneducated, ignorant and fearful fisherman who was later turned into a rock and a great leader, to the point where he walked on water and his shadow could heal the sick, why wouldn't such a person live the rest of his life in submission and obedience to the Man who transformed his life? You would do the same to people who took the chance or risk to believe in you when no one else could. Believing in someone who doesn't appear to be going anywhere in life and giving such a person the opportunity to prove himself is really a great risk; and, in return for giving them that benefit of doubt, that person will end up being loyal to them.

I don't have as much respect for the people who now believe in me and are willing to give me opportunities simply because it's obvious I am going somewhere in life, as for those who saw potential greatness in me and what I could become when no one else did, and staked their resources on me and gave me the opportunities to succeed. That is why I have unyielding, unbreaking and uncompromising loyalty, honour and respect for two major people in my life: my father in the Lord, Rev. Dr Fidelis Ayemoba, who saw me and picked me in the midst of others to serve him as his personal assistant, and in the process my sponsor, Pastor Chijioke Okonkwo, who saw greatness and potentials in me to excel and decided to give me the greatest opportunity I have ever had in all my life to succeed.

'Alone we can do so little; together we can do so much.'
—Helen Keller

To be a great person and leader, you must believe in people because only little things can be achieved individually; but with a great team and concerted efforts and the partnership of others, unimaginable greater things can be achieved. Don't ever underestimate the power of working with a team; your team of people will probably become your greatest asset in life if you wish to accomplish great things. Little people work alone, but great people work with a team. In the words of Helen Keller, 'Alone we can do so little; together we can do so much.' It's people that advance the world, not machines or technology, because everything is an initiative of man through their creative minds.

For instance, a great leader must believe and have confidence in his followers, otherwise they can never give him their best. Business organisations must have belief in their employees for them to do their jobs effectively; if bosses don't believe in their employees, they won't delegate authority to them to exercise some level of authority or the other. By studying the life of the greatest teacher and leader that ever walked on planet Earth, Jesus Christ, we saw how he selected twelve disciples and believed in them enough to delegate authority to them to go out and cast out devils and demons. As the Bible clearly speaks of Him,

And when he had called unto him his twelve disciples, he gave them power against unclean spirits, to cast them out, and to heal all manner of sickness and all manner of disease.
Matthew 10:1

After these things the Lord appointed other seventy also, and sent them two and two before his face into every city and place, whither he himself would come.
Luke 10:1

And more so, when He was about to leave the Earth, He committed His vision to His disciples who were faithful to the end, and that is why we have Christianity today. He believed so much in them that He could delegate so much authority to them to carry out His vision after His departure, as the Bible clearly says,

Go ye therefore, and teach all nations, baptizing them in the name of the Father, and of the Son, and of the Holy Ghost.
Teaching them to observe all things whatsoever I have commanded you: and, lo, I am with you always, even unto the end of the world. Amen.
Matthew 28:19-20

No leader can effectively communicate his vision to his

followers and inspire them enough to buy-into his vision if the leader doesn't believe in them. This is a principle of leadership; if you believe in your followers, they will in return believe in you and give themselves to you. If you don't believe in your team and followers, they will never believe in you; and, if they don't believe in you, your vision will never be actualised, because you will need people to believe in you.

If He didn't believe in the disciples He selected, His mission wouldn't have been executed on Earth. The primary reason he succeeded was because He chose the right team He worked and walked with, but that wouldn't have been possible if He didn't believe in them. To fulfil our destinies on Earth, especially in the world of business, we need to believe in people enough to commit things into their hands and trust them enough to execute them effectively with the least supervision. Don't be deceived; even those that call themselves a self-made billionaire, they didn't give birth to themselves and they didn't print the money in their pockets.

In one way or the other, there will always be the input of some special people who believe in you to give you an opportunity to test your dream, to prove your worth – to show the stuff you are made of – and excel in life. They are called the gift of right men. They could be your parents like, like Sonya Carson, Ben Carson's mother, who inspired him and helped him to believe in himself and built the required self-confidence and belief for success. They could be siblings, family members, colleagues at work, your spouse, friends or even people whom you never knew. You can't excel in life without someone or a group of people who believe in you.

Jesus couldn't have made it on Earth without the twelve disciples who believed in Him, followed Him and gave their lives to Him. Joshua believed in Moses and followed him, Elisha believed in Elija and followed him, the young Timothy believed in Apostle Paul and followed him, Bishop David O. Abioye believes in Bishop David Oyedepo and follows him, the great philosopher Plato believed in Socrates and followed him. Either someone believes in you and invests in you so you can succeed, or people will believe in you and follow you, dedicate their lives to your vision and course, and work for you or with you; and, in doing so, your vision is achieved and their lives are made better. People don't just work for a person or an organisation because of money or they need to job. For instance, I could never work for a human trafficker or drug dealer, or anyone involved in illegal trade regardless of the pay and rewards involved, and I know there are millions of people who feel like that, too. People agree to work for you or with you because of shared values and the belief that they place in you.

So, whichever way, either you are the leader with people following you, or a boss with employees working for you, you get a return or benefit in one way or the other. Alternatively, if someone sees you and decides to help you and invest in you, it's because they believe in you and believe in your potentials, just as in the case of my sponsor, Chijioke Okonkwo, who saw me and believed in me and invested heavily in me to excel.

In life and destiny, you will always need people at different points of your life to fulfil your dreams. In fulfilling destiny, people are basically the critical assets that one will need in order to achieve purpose in life and, until you understand how crucial people are in fulfilling destiny, you may never maximise the usefulness of people. As much as people are great assets in fulfilling destiny, they're also great obstacles and liabilities if you meet the wrong ones. Great people are those who know the power of associations, who have understood the primary goal of people and are wise enough to identify the right people when they see them. For any organisation to be great, they will have to employ the right people to get the job done, for every great accomplishment is usually achieved through human vessels.

For any great organisation, their human resources are their greatest channels by which they excel. Great organisations have great employees. What makes people great and successful largely depends on the quality of people they associate with and work with, so understanding this will help you to be conscious and intentional when it comes to dealing with people. Somebody can walk into your life and, in less than 24 hours, your life will dramatically change for the positive and you see yourself doing excellently well; and someone can also walk into your life and everything you have ever worked for and accumulated will crash and crumble completely.

People we work and associate with will, to a large extent, determine how far we go and achieve in life and destiny, so the quality of lives that we lead depends on the types and quality of people that are in our lives. Great parents raise great children, great businessmen have great associations, great organisations or first-class organisations have first-class employees; and so, everything about life depends on the type of people you work and network with. A poor person could meet a person who could completely turn his or her life around and, in less than 24 hours, such a person's position and financial status will take a new turn, simply because they met someone; you can never underestimate the power of people.

BELIEVE IN THE SUPERNATURAL

I know it is likely for some people to argue with this statement, but I absolutely know that it is correct – there is a life that is higher than the physical life and I so much believe in the supernatural far more than I do the physical, because the physical world is an offspring of the supernatural world. So, the physical is being controlled and manipulated from the realms of the supernatural, and if anyone must amount to something very great and outstanding in the realm of the physical, then it is wise for them to believe in the supernatural and, most importantly, engage or partner with the invisible forces of the supernatural that control the outcomes in the physical.

For me, I believe in God and I serve my Lord Jesus Christ with my whole life and I am eternally committed to Him, to His will, and to the Kingdom, and that is the source of my strength.

Looking back at my life, I cannot but attribute everything happening in my life to my connection with the Immortal One in the invisible realm, because that is where everything emanates from, that is where I draw strength from, and that is where I determine the circumstances of my life in the physical. It is, therefore, wisdom for me or anyone to perpetually remain attached and in partnership with the supernatural.

I am very certain that every great man has a connection in one way or the other to the spiritual world, to some invisible forces that help them in the realm of the physical to do some extraordinary things. In reality, men are helped by spirits; every man is ruled or controlled by one spirit or the other. There is spirit influence over men on Earth and, depending on your connectivity to the invisible realm and, most importantly, to the kind of spirit forces that you are connected to, that will determine the extent of your influence and greatness in the realm of the physical. In the spiritual, spirit forces operate by their ranks, and they can never break their ranks as it's a highly fixed and structured realm; so, depending on the rank of the spirits that you partner with, that will determine the extent and height of the strength that you will exercise and the influence you will make in the physical. Men are helped by spirits; men are ordinary beings who are helped and empowered from the realm of the spirits and from the spirits they are connected to.

And he made in Jerusalem engines, invented by cunning men, to be on the towers and upon the bulwarks, to shoot arrows and great stones withal. And his name spread far abroad; for he was marvellously helped, till he was strong; 2 Chronicles 26:15.

Men are helped in the realm of life by spirit entities. Don't leave your life to chance, don't live an ordinary life, because those who live ordinary lives end up becoming ordinary people and casualties in life. Believe it or not, there are supernatural forces that enable men to do supernatural things on Earth. When you see people doing extraordinary things, consciously or unconsciously, they are being enabled by some extraordinary forces in the realm of the supernatural and that is why I also implore you to be connected to the spiritual realm.

I believe in Jesus, and I believe and know that He is the creator and maker of all things, and therefore He is the highest-ranking personality in the realm of the spirit, because all powers in heaven and on Earth belong to Him and are given to Him. Every other spirit or supernatural force operates in a position far below His power, and how I wish most people knew this and are in partnership with Him by accepting Him as their Lord and personal saviour. I implore you to make Him your Lord and personal saviour if you haven't already. Receive Him into your life, let Him come and rule in your heart, and you will see what greatness He will make out of your life. If you know where I'm coming from and who I used to be before Jesus came into my life, and the awesome and amazing transformation going on in my life, then you will be able to glorify God in me and believe that, indeed, there is a power, grace and supernatural force that really can make men great in life. I hereby introduce you to Him, who is the Lord of all and the God of all. He is the Jesus Christ, the saviour of the world.

THE MAN AT THE POOL OF BETHESDA

There is the story of the man who had been at the pool of Bethesda for 38 years, when Jesus walked up to him and asked him if he wanted to be healed. Instead of a straight yes or no, the man decided to give a background story of his predicament. As much as that answer was off-point, it revealed something very powerful and interesting: he said,

'Sir, **I HAVE NO MAN,** when the water is troubled, to put me into the pool: but while I am coming, another steppeth down before me.

John 5:7

That when the water was troubled, before he could enter, another person entered. Meaning, others made it before him because they had men-helpers, expressing the point that his reason for stagnation for too long was because he didn't have men to help him, or that the type of men he had were also handicapped and incapacitated like him, so they couldn't help, either. This also reveals that every man in one way or the other is incapacitated to do a particular thing and would, therefore, require the services of other men, because God never created man to be self-sufficient.

FOUR TYPES OF PEOPLE YOU WILL INTERACT WITH IN DESTINY

If you are ever going to fulfil your purpose and maximise your destiny in life, you are going to interact with four basic types of people. T.D. Jakes identified three of them and I will add the fourth type to the list, as identified by T.D Jakes:

1. Confidants
2. Constituents
3. Comrades
4. Conductors

According to T.D. Jakes, the first and the most important person you will meet in the journey of life is a confidant. Confidants are divine destiny helpers that God will send your way to help and support you in life until you fulfil your destiny. They are for you and into you; they were primarily sent to you for the purpose of carrying your cross and lightening your burden in life. In other words, they are burden bearers. Destiny is a great burden to bear and God knows you can't bear the burden of destiny alone. Destiny is a great responsibility that requires a lot of sacrifices for it to be fulfilled – and, believe me, you don't want to carry the burden alone and pay the price all by yourself.

Confidants are those who stand by you through the thick and thin. If you mess up, they are still there for you; if you

IF YOU MUST SUCCEED, BELIEVE IN YOURSELF

fail, they are there to encourage you. It doesn't matter what you do, their hearts are with you. They have your back and watch your back, and when others leave you because of your mistakes, they will stick with you. They are more interested in your success and progress than in anything else. They are custom designed for you and with you and inseparably integrated in your life; they challenge you to excel, they motivate and inspire you to move beyond your limits, to stretch beyond your comfort zone. They see the future in you and are committed to helping you bring it out. Even when you can't see a beautiful, glorious future in you and ahead of you, they help you to see it; they point the future out to you and tell you why you must get there. While others castigate and critique you, and tell you countless reasons why you can't make it, confidants will comfort you and tell you one good reason why you *can* make it.

Most times, confidants may not be related to you and they stick closer to you than your own family relatives; they sacrifice for you and give up so much just to see you succeed. The best summary of them is 'they believe in you and are committed to making the best out of you'. The challenge is, they are very few in life; you may just have one of them in your whole life, but if you are blessed and privileged, you may have two or three. Just one alone can have the capacity of 20 million people in your life, as one confidant can do what 10 million people in your life can't do for you.

Imagine having two or three of such people! In my life, Pastor Chijioke Okonkwo is a perfect example. I remember the first destination he wanted me to go to carry out my studies was Canada; however, when I secured admission into one of the universities in Canada, I was refused a Visa and, after many attempts, everything proved abortive. He went out of his way to pay an agent to do it, and had already paid part of the school fees deposit as required by the institution, but all to no avail. Instead of giving up or backing out, he said to me one day, 'I am particularly interested in your case.'

That is how confidants talk, they don't leave and abandon you when things are tough and not working out; they stand strong and back you. I thought he would have backed out as Canada didn't work out, even though the deposit we had made was not refunded, he still didn't mind. He went ahead to seek another alternative, and a better one, just to make sure I achieve my dream and fulfil my destiny.

The second set of people you will interact with in your journey to your destiny is constituents. The constituents are not with you, or for you, but are into what you are for. They are with you because of similar interests, not necessarily because of you. And once they achieve their goal, or even find someone with a better offer, they switch camps. They are with you for the purpose of their own interests, what they can get from you, how they can further their lives by associating with you, and immediately their interests are achieved they will walk away. They are always ready to work and walk with you as long as their interests will be met; everything is all about them and their interests.

You must be wise when dealing with constituents because they are always part of your team or organisation; but whenever a course of action or activity is no longer of benefit or profit to them, or help them achieve their interest, they will no longer give their best, and some may even opt out! Everything is all about them, their interests and desires, so they are always looking for where the pasture is greener; they are always looking out for a fence where it's greener and fresher on the other side, and if they meet another person with a better offer and deal, they will walk away. To them, life is all about what they can get, not what they can give; and the fact is, you will meet many of them, for they are aplenty. It was John F. Kennedy that said, 'Ask not what your country can do for you – ask what you can do for your country.' For the constituents, however, it's all about 'What can he do for me?', 'What can they do for me?', 'What can the country do for me?', 'What can this organisation do for me?' Life is all about them!

IF YOU MUST SUCCEED, BELIEVE IN YOURSELF

It's toxic to build your life around these people, so be very discerning as to why someone is in your life, or why you are also in someone else's life. You will always have them in your life, as they are always in everyone's life, but never think they are there for you. These people are like politicians who say, 'No permanent friend or enemies, but permanent interests.' Just like when a politician who has power and influence always has many supporters and followers around him, but immediately he loses the election and falls from position of influence, all those supporters and followers abandon him for the new one who has ascended to a greater height. I don't only pray for my destiny helpers to find me; I also pray that I might meet those whom I can help and become their destiny helper! It's important to understand that we live by giving, we become great by making others great; we are helped by helping others, and we rise by lifting others. Life is all about giving and making meaningful contributions, and that is how to live a rich, fulfilled and satisfied life.

The third group of people you will encounter in life is the comrades. The comrades are with you temporarily, because there is a common enemy both of you have in common; they want to team up with you to overcome the enemy, and afterwards they are gone from you. They are against what you are against, so it's easier to team up with you not out of love and respect for you, but to have the enemy defeated, or to have a complex puzzle or task dissolved.

For instance, imagine living in a neighbourhood where there is power outage or environmental challenge, or where you receive an unjust bill from the landlord or landlady and would require a concerted effort to surmount such a situation. A comrade who has never greeted you, or knocked at your door to check up on you for years, will suddenly come knocking at your door, and calling on you for a collaboration in order to solve the problem at hand, because they are against the same challenge and are not comfortable with the situation.

Their main target is just to solve a specific problem and

walk away, not seeking a long-term friendship or teamwork. They don't care what happens to you once the problem is solved. They behave like scaffolding.

Immediately the purpose is accomplished, the scaffolding is removed. Their goal was to accomplish a task and move away; they are ready to give you their unreserved and unsolicited support, because the primary task at hand is also their main concern. Sometimes, they may not be the one to initiate the solution process.

They may see you attempting to solve a particular problem that has been giving them headache, but never knew how to go about it; then they willingly come to submit and pledge their support to assist you in overcoming the problem and, afterwards, they are gone. You never see them again because the pain is gone. However, you don't have to be angry when the scaffolding is removed because you already have your building erected and completed.

The fourth type of people I found out about and added to the three identified by T.D. Jakes is what I call the conductors. The conductors are strategic people positioned at different junctures in your path of destiny; they are strategic helpers that you meet at different points in life and their primary assignment or goal is to offer you direction or assist you to get to the next point of your destiny or career. They are temporal and seasonal; they don't last long, or follow you to where you are going. They are divine also, and sent by God just like the confidants, but the difference is that confidants are with you to help you for life; they go with you through the thick and thin, they support you and are always there to help. The conductors, on the other hand, are not always there.

You probably will not see them again after the first encounter because you were on transit; you will always meet them on transit and they render their support and assistance in order to transit you from your current position to the next bus stop of life. They are like a vehicle that conveys you from one bus stop and drops you at another bus stop, from

IF YOU MUST SUCCEED, BELIEVE IN YOURSELF

where you will either get to your destination or may have to seek further help to get you to your destination. Most times, they are new acquaintances, while other times they may be strangers; but one thing is certain – they will end up helping you to get to the next juncture of your career and destiny, and you will always remember your encounter with them.

They are like the scaffolding in the sense that when they play their part in your life, they walk away because you people were on transit and probably heading towards different destinations, so they were never meant to stay long. For instance, I was once on a flight to London and the passenger next to me was on a connecting flight to India. Just imagine being on a connecting flight to London and you meet someone on the same flight also connecting to India, and the person shared an experience or information with you that changed your life for the best and you never saw the person again. That is an example.

I remember my first trip to London. I took a connecting flight to Doha, Qatar and on the same flight was a teenage student connecting to India for her studies. Before we boarded, her parents walked up to me and handed her to me and pleaded that I support and guide her along the journey. At the border, she had a problem with the immigration control and I had to come to her rescue. I helped her and, after the problem was rectified, she sat next to me on the plane. Everything I did for her was within that short period of time and it ended there. Whatever happened to her after we parted ways at the airport, I don't know and I probably wouldn't recognise her again if I were to meet her later in life. If you observe well, you will realise there are people who have helped you in times past, or who you have helped at one point or the other, but you can't remember them, or even say what happened to them afterwards. Conductors are like the signposts on the path of destiny pointing you in the right direction, but they never go with you. To fulfil destiny in a grand style, we need them and, most especially, the confidants. These two in particular help to fast forward our journey in life and enable us to arrive on time.

Change your thoughts and you change your world.
–Norman Vincent Peale

CHAPTER EIGHT
THE POWER OF MENTAL OVERHAULING

'You begin to fly when you let go of self-limiting beliefs and allow your mind and aspirations to rise to greater heights.'
—Brian Tracy

So many people are hindered in life because they are filled with self-debilitating beliefs and self-doubts, among other factors, which place a limitation on people's potentials for success. Self-doubts destroy your confidence and courage in your ability and capacity to achieve your dreams in life, but in order to rise and soar in life you will have to conquer every symptom of self-doubt. Self-doubt destroys self-esteem and self-value; people who doubt themselves never find the inner strength and confidence to chase their dreams because it will always make you feel inferior and incapable. Self-doubt is a monster that sets limitations on people's path of progress. When ideas come to your mind, and you begin to question your capability and qualifications to make those ideas a reality, you are allowing the spirit of self-doubt to stop you.

For anyone who desires to build a healthy self-image and esteem, the first thing to conquer is self-doubt, because that and self-esteem are two antithetical phenomena, they can't work together. A lot of people develop self-doubts because of negative criticism and different kinds of abuse, but if you are going to excel in life you will have to rise above the negative public opinion of you. No one knows you better than you do and no one can give an accurate description of yourself better than you. You are the one to develop the personality you want to be, it's your responsibility to decide the kind of a person you want to be. Waiting for public approval and

Believe in Yourself

affirmation from people before you believe in yourself is an effort in futility, because the world is full of people who are hurting, who know how to criticise and not compliment, and how to condemn and not console. To be great, you must learn to be comfortable with criticism, because it will come.

BREAKING SELF-IMPOSED LIMITATIONS

Many people are hindered in life by what they refer to as limitations of life; but, inadvertently, true limitations of life are not those that are external, but internal. True disabilities are those of the human mind, the ones you placed on yourself as a disability. Like the Indian Chef Vikas Khanna rightly said, 'Disability is the inability to see ability'. The real disability is internal or within, never without. People are actually disabled by their thoughts, which is the fountain from where man's abilities and inabilities proceed from.

'Disability is the inability to see ability.'
—*Vikas Khanna*

Everything proceeds from the human mind, the factory of life where civilisation and all human advancement and progress emanate from. The mind of man is the production centre where everyone generates their lots in life. According to Napoleon Hill, there are no limitations to the mind except those we acknowledge. Both poverty and riches are the offspring of thought. A person will eventually be disabled in the outside world his because life is lived from within. While everyone's life on the external is a reflection of what and who they are in the internal, the external circumstances of a person's life are the reflection of their inner state; therefore, your external world is a mirror that reflects your internal world.

A person who is perpetually poor can't be said to be different from the poverty thoughts that dominate

'There are no limitations to the mind except those we acknowledge. Both poverty and riches are the offspring of thought.'
—*Napoleon Hill*

THE POWER OF MENTAL OVERHAULING

his or her mind, because our external circumstances are a direct reflection of our internal mind. The same way a physical mirror reflects and gives an accurate interpretation of someone's physical facial appearance, the same way our conditions and circumstances are the mirrors that reflect and interpret our mental conditions. They are the dominant thoughts of the human mind, because life was designed to be lived inside-out, or from within. So, if you see people perpetually poor, it is because they either believe they are poor and can't do anything about it, or they believe they were destined to be poor. Whichever is right, their poverty can't be unconnected to their thoughts. In life, every one of us will eventually evolve to become what we believe.

As the world revolves around man's continuous thinking, so do our conditions and circumstances revolve around our thoughts, because all the developments and civilisation of mankind are direct consequence of man's thoughts.

If you interview a rich man or woman, or ever hear them talk, pay attention to their words and you will discover the difference between the language of the poor and that of the rich. And remember, of course, that words proceed from the mind.

'We will always evolve to become what we believe.'

So, everyone's status or position in life is directly connected to their thoughts and mind. It doesn't matter the ugly circumstances or contrary circumstances of a man; if he consistently and continually thinks about riches and prosperity, the contrary circumstances on the external will eventually be altered to correspond with the controlling thoughts of his mind.

'As the world revolves around man's continuous thinking, so do our conditions and circumstances revolve around our thoughts.'

Alternatively, if you give a man who is poor in his mind one million dollars, give him a couple of years and his external circumstance, which currently seems to be rich, will eventually change to correspond to the dominant thoughts in his mind. By this principle, circumstances will unfold in which he will misuse the money and eventually return back to the poverty equilibrium of his mind. If the equilibrium of someone's mind is on poverty, it doesn't matter how much you give to them; by the law of equilibrium, everything a person has on the outside will tilt to align and correspond to the state of poverty equilibrium in their mind.

I have personally observed this principle in the life of one of my first cousins, who is a lawyer. He has always lived in poverty and believed that most people would engage in unlawful acts to be rich; so I have always known him to beg from people, even as a lawyer, because he wouldn't strive to work hard and be rich, yet was very sound in cerebral knowledge. Then suddenly, after living in poverty for years, a few years ago he stumbled upon a huge amount of money. He sold some land and made a profit of 6 million naira ($40,000). I remember calling him to ask him to lend me some money to publish my first book, which he declined. Instead, he used the money to buy three different cars and went cruising around everywhere. Eventually, exactly six months later, he called me to beg me for some money. In six months, all the money he'd made was gone and he returned back to the poverty equilibrium of the mind that reflected his life before the money came.

Really, poverty and riches are all offspring of the mind, as our conditions in life are somewhat connected to our mind and the way we think. In the long haul, our external circumstances will always adjust to correspond to the internal equilibrium of the state of our minds, whether good or bad, poverty or prosperity. So, in order to correct any situation of life, we need to correct the internal thought pattern that has created it.

CONQUER THESE DESTRUCTIVE MINDSETS

1. SETTLING-FOR-LESS MINDSET

This kind of mindset is actually evidence of someone who doesn't truly believe in themselves and in their possibilities for greatness. This kind of thought pattern makes one live below average, even when they are super qualified for a good job, as they always want to accept something lesser than they deserve. Leading this kind of lifestyle will deny you of good things and better opportunities in life, because if someone observes that you are such a person, they will always take undue advantage of you. This is the major cause of exploitation – if people known you to always be the lamb for the slaughter and sacrifice, they will always exploit you and deny you what you actually deserve, because they know you won't do anything about it.

If you really want to lead a good-quality life, never settle for less. I am not saying you shouldn't start small and grow in life. We all started small before attaining great heights, but not settling for less means knowing what you truly deserve. Having paid your dues and necessary requirements, you should never settle for less because, eventually, you will be comfortable with the idea of being lesser than everyone else.

2. 'WHITE-COLLAR JOBS FOR WHITES AND BLUE-COLLAR JOBS FOR BLACKS' MINDSET

I understand what it means to live in a foreign land, especially if you are coloured. A black woman who has been in the UK long before I came here told me I had to work extra hard to make both ends meet. I don't have a problem with that, because wherever you are in this world, whether in your own homeland or abroad, you must work hard to be successful. But my challenge with her statement was that, to be successful as a black in a foreign nation, I must work hard because, as she said, the best-paying jobs are reserved for the whites and the

Believe in Yourself

indigenes, while the menial jobs are reserved for the blacks. Therefore, most blacks have to work at five or six different jobs just to get by and have their bills paid and needs met! I said to her, 'I don't believe in that! It's not true, ma'am!'

I then told her that, back in her own country, the whites still work and occupy high positions while the blacks work at menial jobs; so, the problem is not racism, but mentality and self-development. It's rather unfortunate that many blacks still have the slavery mentality; they still think other people are responsible for their failure and poverty. Most of African nations still think that their colonial masters are responsible for their underdevelopment, which is not true. If you have to succeed, you must eliminate the thought that the good jobs belong to a particular set of people, while the low-paying jobs belong to a set of people because of the colour of their skin. If you are ever going to excel in life, you must believe your future is in your hands to decide; you must decide what you want and go for it.

> *Nobody was created to control and decide the outcome of your life.*

Nobody was created to control and decide the outcome of your life. I know a Nigerian, in fact my own Pastor where I worship, who occupies a high position among the whites where he works. He actually got the job from Nigeria, all expenses paid for him, with diplomatic benefits, no tax, and no restrictions whatsoever. He was flown here to attend the interview among the white folks and he got the job. They pay him so highly, his family are here with him and everything was paid for. I then asked the woman, if the Pastor could get such a very high-paying job all the way from Nigeria, how could she say that 'The best and high-paying jobs belong to the whites, while the bad and low-paying jobs belong to the blacks?' If you live and work in a foreign land and you have this mindset, the odds are you will never rise to greatness and maximise your potentials because you have placed a limitation on what you can achieve.

3. DISADVANTAGED MINDSET

Another type of destructive mindset that you will have to overcome is a disadvantaged mentality, by thinking you are inadequate, unqualified or disadvantaged because of your background, race, sex, or religion, or even physical disability. Any form of thought that makes you feel you are disadvantaged will rob you of your possibilities and chances of becoming successful in life. Never think someone else is better than you simply because of their family background, race or country.

No one in life ever had the opportunity to choose where to be born, or the family to be born into, but we all determine and decide where we want to end up. So, every great person on Earth chose to be great; no one is actually great because they were born into a great family or come from a certain nation, because I have seen beggars, even in the richest nations of the world. If you go to the richest and most prosperous countries, you will still find poor people; and there are people who were born into wealthy families who squandered all their family fortunes and eventually ended up poor and committed suicide. So, whatever family you were born into or the nation you come from, it does not what determine whether you will be rich or not, successful or not, or prosperous or not. There are people in Africa who are richer than many people in great nations like the USA, UK, France, Canada etc. In order to maximise your potentials and become great, never believe or think you are disadvantaged. Like big brother Pastor Chijioke Okonkwo said to me, 'There are no spaces anywhere, you have to create your own space.'

If no one gives you a platform to showcase your talent, why

> *No one in life ever had the opportunity to choose where to be born, or the family to be born into, but we all determine and decide where and how we want to end up*

not create one for yourself? If no one gives you an opportunity, why not create one for yourself? You are not disadvantaged in any way. Those things you think are your disadvantages, you analyse them critically; they are your advantages in disguise, the reasons why you are going to succeed.

4. SLAVERY MINDSET

This is the worst of them all and mother of all destructive mindsets. Slavery mindset is what makes people small all their lives. Such a mindset that keeps people in bondage and mental slavery is worse than physical slavery. In my opinion, the African nations are in a worse type of slavery than during the era of the colonial masters and slave trade. There is nothing as terrible as mental slavery; it makes you think everyone is responsible for your problems, and makes you believe that your success and progress is in the hands of other people, whether individuals or nations. This is the kind of mindset that tells you someone is better off than you, that you can't fulfil your dreams for whatever reasons; it makes you think you need someone's approval before you can succeed; it makes you think your life and destiny is in the hands of someone; it makes you put all your hopes and expectations into someone. It makes you serve people continually because you believe that, if they don't help you, no one else will.

Such type of mindset is prevalent in Africa and that is the reason for the abject poverty. I have walked out on people who never expected I would. For example, my former boss used to threaten his workers that, should we leave his company, we would end up begging in the street because of the high unemployment rate. I actually quit without a salary and without first getting another job, but I went on to begin my own company and started making money, far more than I could ever have saved while working for him. Two years later, I left the country. But when I left the job, everyone insulted me and called it a foolish decision.

There are millions of people out there who are afraid to step out into uncharted territory because they have been sold the biggest lie of the century: that they are disadvantaged in one way or the other, or that they are not qualified to attain a particular height, or get to a certain position in life. Believing that your future or success is in the hands of anyone including your parents, bosses, country or friends is a great lie. Arise, and shake off the slavery mentality and let loose your life and destiny. Let loose your mind from captivity and bondage of wrong beliefs and thought, and soar unto unimaginable heights that await you and which you never thought possible.

Some Inspirational Quotes on Self-limitations
The only limits you have are the limits you believe. (Wayne Dyer)

You can't escape from a prison until you recognise you are in one. People who have chosen to live within the limits of their old beliefs continue to have the same experiences. It takes effort and commitment to break old patterns. (Bob Proctor)

Man often becomes what he believes himself to be. If I keep on saying to myself that I cannot do a certain thing, it is possible that I may end by really becoming incapable of doing it. On the contrary, if I have the belief that I can do it, I shall surely acquire the capacity to do it even if I may not have it at the beginning. (Mahatma Gandhi)

There is one grand lie - that we are limited. The only limits we have are the limits we believe. (Wayne Dyer)

We learn our belief systems as very little children, and then we move through life creating experiences to match our beliefs. Look back in your own life and notice how often you have gone through the same experience. (Louise Hay)

You begin to fly when you let go of self-limiting beliefs and allow your mind and aspirations to rise to greater heights. (Brian Tracy)

If you raise your standards but don't really believe you can meet them, you've already sabotaged yourself. You won't even try; you'll be lacking the sense of certainty that allows you to tap the deepest capacity that's within you... Our beliefs are like unquestioned commands, telling us how things are, what's possible and impossible and what we can and can not do. They shape every action, every thought and every feeling that we experience. As a result, changing our belief systems is central to making any real and lasting change in our lives. (Tony Robbins)

You have the power in the present moment to change limiting beliefs and consciously plant the seeds for the future of your choosing. As you change your mind, you change your experience. (Serge King)

Never let the limitations or insecurities of others limit what is possible for you. (Hal Elrod)

Do just once what others say you can't do, and you will never pay attention to their limitations again. (James Cook)

If you accept a limiting belief, then it will become a truth for you. (Louise Hay)

All it takes is one person in any generation to heal a family's limiting beliefs. (Gregg Braden)

Don't limit yourself. Many people limit themselves to what they think they can do. You can go as far as your mind lets you. What you believe, remember, you can achieve. (Mary Kay Ash)

The human body is capable of amazing physical deeds. If we could just free ourselves from our perceived limitations and tap into our internal fire, the possibilities are endless. (Dean Karnazes)

All too often we're filled with negative and limiting beliefs. We're filled with doubt. We're filled with guilt or with a sense unworthiness. We have a lot of assumptions about the way vorld is that are actually wrong. (Jack Canfield)

I'm not interested in your limiting beliefs, I'm interested in what makes you limitless. (Brendon Burchard)

Many people are passionate, but because of their limiting beliefs about who they are and what they can do, they never take actions that could make their dream a reality. (Tony Robbins)

Do the uncomfortable. Become comfortable with these acts. Prove to yourself that your limiting beliefs die a quick death if you will simply do what you feel uncomfortable doing. (Darren Rowse)

At the core of One Spirit Medicine is the idea that how we perceive the world 'out there' is a projection of internal maps that shape our beliefs and guide how we think, feel and behave. These maps are the unconscious programs that drive our experience of life and the state of our health. The key to optimum health is to upgrade these unconscious maps and limiting beliefs that have been driving us to a toxic lifestyle and relationships. (Alberto Villoldo)

Chronic self-doubt is a symptom of the core belief, 'I'm not good enough.' We adopt these types of limiting beliefs in response to our family and childhood experiences, and they become rooted in the subconscious... we have the ability to take action to override it. (Lauren Mackler)

Know that all the limiting beliefs from your family, your friends, your fears and the world will begin to come up once you start to take action. Move through them. This part of the process is where we begin to grow as individuals into who we were meant to be by challenging all of these limiting beliefs and fears. (Mastin Kipp)

'Believe it can be done. When you believe something can be done, really believe, your mind will find the ways to do it. Believing a solution paves the way to solution.'
—David J. Schwartz, The Magic of Thinking Big

CHAPTER NINE
IF YOU MUST SUCCEED, BELIEVE IN YOUR IDEAS AND DREAM

'Many people will not believe in you and it's normal with life; but if you must be successful, you must believe in yourself.'

The beauty of life is making continuous progress and success in what you do regardless of how little it may seem. Life was designed to be progressive, so making progress and advancement is normal in life, but stagnation is abnormal. Remaining at one spot in life is abnormal, even God abhors it. When the children of Israel had stayed for too long on a particular spot, God who created life to be progressive abhorred the situation and came to force them to move forward.

Here is the account in Deuteronomy 1:6-7:

The LORD our God spake unto us in Horeb, saying, Ye have dwell long enough in this mount:

Turn you, and take your journey, and go to the mount of the Amorites, and unto all the places nigh thereunto, in the plain, in the hills, and in the vale, and in the south, and by the sea side...

Have you ever wondered why God had to create all the parts of the human body to be facing front and forward? Notice that no part of the human body was fixed at the back or to face backwards! All the parts of the body are facing forward and that implies that everyone is meant to be moving forward in life, because making progress consistently and intermittently is supposed to be normal with life. Remaining on a particular spots or position in life for too long than is necessary is abnormal and you will have to fight against whatever it is that keeps you stagnated for too long on the spot.

Believe in Yourself

In order to succeed in life you must have goals, because one of the major catalysts for making progress and advancements in life is setting goals. Dreamers change the world! An impactful life is all about having dreams to fulfil and it's only in fulfilling your dreams that you make progress and advancement in life. A life without dreams is boring and meaningless, and such a life is not worth living. Martin Luther King Jr. was right when he said, 'If a man has no purpose for living, he is not fit to live'. A life without dreams and aspirations is a dead life, because dead things cannot dream; only living things can see ahead. Every great person on Earth is a person of great dreams and desire for significance; anyone whoever accomplished anything great in life did so because they dared to dream big. Dreaming big and pursuing your dreams is evidence that you truly believe in yourself, as only those who believe in themselves can actually dream big. Helen Keller was absolutely right when she noted:

> *'The only thing worse than being blind is having eyes but no vision.'*

If you desire to advance and make progress in life from one level to an another, then you must be a man or woman of dreams. Dreaming big has to be a part of your life, because dreams create passion and passion is the fuel that drives you to fulfil your dreams. When I see depressed people in life, I see people who never have a compelling dream; because compelling dreams usually come with passion, and it is this passion that keeps you going when the going gets tough until you reach your destination and achieve your dream.

Depression is not a characteristic of life; rather, it's a consequence of a position or attitude of life that someone assumes. In other words, it's a consequence or outcome of the position of life that one takes. People don't just stay and become depressed; rather, it's usually the result of leading an empty life, a purposeless and dreamless life, a life without contribution and significance. If people don't have a reason to live and

> *'Depression is a consequence of a purposeless and dreamless life'*

lack the excitement and eagerness of waking up each morning, they will naturally be depressed. Depression is, therefore, a consequence of a purposeless and dreamless life. Not eagerly looking forward to something significant and worthwhile in the future is a bad disposition towards life and the outcome will eventually become depression.

Purpose births passion and passion births power for pursuit

Purpose births passion and passion births power for pursuit An optimistic and energised life is evidence of a purposeful life. People with dreams and aspirations are always joyful and full of excitement and extraordinary energy, even in the midst of overwhelming odds. To bring people out of depression, give them a hope to live for, a cause for hope and something to look forward to. It's our dreams that make us wake up early in the morning and keep us up late at night; dreamers are never discouraged by the ugly circumstances and conditions of life. Only people who don't explore life become very small and ordinary. Life is an adventure and everyone is supposed to be adventurous; this is the excitement and joy of living.

'To bring people out of depression, give them a hope to live for, a cause for hope and something to look forward to'

Helen Keller couldn't have been more correct when she noted, **'Life is either a daring adventure or nothing at all.'**

Limited by Your Visions and Dreams

Genesis 13:14, ...as far as your eyes can see, to you will I give it to.

Every one of us on Earth is limited by the size of our dreams and visions, for no individual can ever rise beyond the level of their dreams; there is no one that can rise above the boundaries and limitations of his or her dreams and vision in life. It's our dreams that define and determine the extent to which we can go in life, because no one can go further

> *No man or woman can rise beyond the level of his or her dream and imagination*

than he can dream; no one can go beyond the finish line of his visions and aspirations in life. No one can achieve beyond the imaginations of his heart, no one can ever achieve beyond what he or she can conceive within their hearts or minds, because this is where the boundaries of life are set; for the limitations of a person's life are those that are found in the depth of their mind, and inside the human mind contains the limitations of a man. No person is actually handicapped on the outside of him, but the true handicap and limitations of a man are those that are found in the contents of his mind. That is why the Bible says:

Keep thy heart with all diligence; for out of it are the issues of life.

Proverbs 4:23

Success comes from the heart, victory comes from the heart, progress comes from the heart; everything you will ever desire in life is already within you. Riches are inside of you, success is inside of you, and greatness lies within you, not outside. That is the reason why you have no business competing with anyone, because all you seek is within you. Poverty comes from within you and, likewise, prosperity, for a person is first poor within before they are poor without; everything you see in the physical is what you produced from within you, and if you must change the circumstances of your life then you have to change what you are manufacturing and producing within your mind.

The heart is your manufacturing plant or room, your heart is your workshop where you create, produce

> *It's our dreams that define and determine the extent to which we can go in life, for no one can go farther than he can dream; no one can go beyond the finish line of his visions and aspirations in life*

IF YOU MUST SUCCEED, BELIEVE IN YOUR IDEAS AND DREAM

and assemble everything you desire in life, and from there they are transported into the physical reality of your world. So, everything you have was produced by you in the centre of your heart and manifested into your physical reality by your words and actions.

Therefore, both good and bad, success and failure, life and death, prosperity and poverty, advancements and stagnation are all found within the heart of an individual. Life proceeds from the heart, true life is in the heart of a man and that is where everything emanates from.

> *A good man out of the good treasure of the heart bringeth forth good things: and an evil man out of the evil treasure bringeth forth evil things.*
> *Matthew 12:35*

If a person sees himself to be poor, he or she will definitely end up a poor person; if anyone dreams and sees himself or herself to be a failure, such a person will be nothing but a failure; whoever sees himself or herself as a great person, there is no force in the universe that can make the person end up as mediocre. Whatever you see yourself becoming is what you will certainly become, because the universe was designed with supernatural forces, both positive and negative, that usually align in a direction that is consistent with the dreams and constant thoughts of a man in order to see to it that all the thoughts and imaginations of a man come into practical fulfilment and manifestation. There are invisible forces in the universe and the purpose of these forces is to align with the motives, visions, aspirations and dominant thoughts of a person's heart to empower them for physical realisation.

It's important to note that the physical world is not as physical as you think it is; there are laws that are put into it to govern the operations of every person's

> *Success comes from the heart, victory comes from the heart, progress comes from the heart; everything you will ever desire in life is already within you.*

Believe in Yourself

activity on Earth; there are forces that are built into the physical world to govern its operation such that it cannot be unjustly and wrongly manipulated by anyone. This is the reason behind the statement that success doesn't happen by chance or luck; chance or luck are not the guiding principles of forces that are put into operation in the universe to govern the Earth, otherwise everyone would offer up their life to chance.

> *By the operation of the principle of Cause and Effect, every one of us has become the master of our fate and the captain of our destiny.*

The Earth was designed to operate by the principle of cause and effect, meaning that everything is made to happen by a force or cause of action and, by this universal law, God has made everyone the captain and architect of their destiny. We are all the masters of our fate; we determine the outcome and possibilities of our lives on Earth by the decision and actions we take daily.

It's expensive to live your life governed by chance and expect that you will succeed, because no one has ever accomplished anything of great value in life by chance. Chance is not one of the principles of the universe. Success is intentional, and never by chance! If people would dream and believe in their dreams and think consistently on their dreams, they would create the pathway and vent through which the positive forces of the universe will align with the thoughts of their hearts to bring their dreams into fulfilment. If you dream negatively (cause), you will create the portal through which negative forces will align with your negative thoughts and imaginations to produce negative outcomes (effects). Alternatively, if you dream, think and imagine positively you will also create the portals through which the positive forces of the universe will align with your positive thoughts and imaginations in your heart to translate them into the physical reality. Therefore, everyone is a product of their thought and imagination. Every one of us is forged in the constant and dominant thoughts and imaginations of our hearts.

> *We are all shaped and forged in the thoughts and imaginations of our hearts. We are, therefore, the offspring and products of our hearts.*

Remember, 'dreaming' is not a physical phenomenon; it's a spiritual activity. Dreams are supernatural forces and possess the power to manifest themselves in the physical. You don't see 'dreams' until they are turned into physical realities. Dreams are spiritual forces and the spiritual controls the physical. Every spiritual force has inherent power to manifest itself in the realm of the physical, and there is no physical element or force that has enough power to hinder the manifestation of a spiritual phenomenon or force. The physical world was created from the spiritual world and by a spirit which is God. The world (physical) was created by the Word (spiritual) according to Hebrews 11:1:

Through faith we understand that the worlds were framed by the word of God, so that things which are seen are were not made of things which do appear.

The physical world was not designed to control the spiritual because the physical world is an offspring of the spiritual world; so, the physical world can be controlled by the elements and forces of the spiritual or supernatural. Fortunately, 'dreams', 'words', 'thoughts' and 'imaginations' are elements and forces of the spiritual or supernatural and can never be stopped by any physical element in the universe.

TAKING CONTROL OF YOUR LIFE
There are five forces I call the forces of life. They shape the outcome of your life on Earth and, in order to take control of your life and destiny, you must take control of these

Believe in Yourself

five forces. Whoever controls these forces in your life, automatically controls your life and future. They are:
1. Thoughts
2. Words
3. Dreams
4. Imagination
5. Faith

These five forces are so powerful that they shape our lives consciously or unconsciously. They are supernatural elements and can't be controlled or hindered by the physical elements or forces in the physical real. The question is not whether you engage them or not in your life, but *how* you engage them. Everybody is always relating and interacting with them in one form or the other, whether consciously or unconsciously and positively or negatively; and it is the results of those interactions that have shaped people's lives and conditions.

THOUGHTS:
For as he thinketh in his heart, so is he...
Proverbs 23:7

> *Whether you think you can or you think you can't, you're right.*
> *Henry Ford*

Unbeknown to many people, our thoughts constantly shape our lives, so the question is: 'What do they think about most of the time?' Many people are thinking negatively and ignorantly and that is why their lives are full of negative circumstances and conditions. Even a deaf, dumb and blind person can think, and it's in their thoughts that their lives are shaped.

WORDS:
Death and life are in the power of the tongue: and they that love it shall eat the fruit thereof.
Proverbs 18:21

IF YOU MUST SUCCEED, BELIEVE IN YOUR IDEAS AND DREAM

...the words that I speak unto you, they are spirit and they are life.

John 6:63

For he that will love life, and see good days, let him refrain his tongue from evil, and his lips that they speak no guile.
1Peter 3:10

Words are spirit, they don't die. They are invisible forces that manifest physically and shape the conditions of people's lives. Many people have unconsciously designed their lives and conditions by the words they speak every day. And, again, it's not about whether people are talking or not, but what are they saying because everyone speaks.

> *Your words are your own self-fulfilling prophecy*

Virtually all the time, it's the thoughts in people's hearts that are turned into words, which later are propelled into actions, and in turn form their attitudes that shape their habits and, eventually, form their character; and it's your character that determines who you become and what you are in life. So many folks have unconsciously spoken their failure and death. Your words are your own prophecy some people go about looking for who will give them prophecy, not knowing that they are their own greatest prophet. It is the words they speak to themselves and about themselves that are the prophecies of their own destinies; so, if they have spoken wrong words, they have inadvertently prophesied wrong things into their lives and they will eventually see the fulfilment of their own negative prophecies. Words are powerful, more powerful than anything you can ever imagine in the universe.

Have you ever thought about this, that most if not all the conflicts between people, and even wars that broke out between nations, were as a result of words that were spoken? Have you ever imagined why people respond to words and statements? Have you ever been angry and at the verge of reacting, when suddenly someone spoke some inspiring and

> *'Everyman is the 'script-actor' of his own words'*

gentle words to you that calmed you and dispelled all the negative emotions and energy that were about to cause you to react? Have you been in a situation where you didn't want to do something and someone came to you and spoke some grace-filled words, words that were seasoned with salt that changed your mind and made you do what you never wanted to do? Can you ever imagine the kind of words that some people or leaders spoke and commanded many followers that laid down their lives for them? What kind of power and energy was in such words that could make people give up their course, dreams and careers just to follow someone, even to the point of losing their own lives? Think about it!

Words are the most powerful forces in the universe that shape people's lives and destiny, so be careful of the words you speak to yourself because you will be the one to act out the script of your own words, for every man is the script-actor of his own words. You will definitely be the one to act out the script of your life, which you have written by your own words.

DREAMS AND IMAGINATION
...and now nothing shall be restrained from them which they have imagined to do.
Genesis 11:6

Much has been said about dreaming. The dreams you have, your hopes and expectations, will most likely come to pass if you hold onto them. When people go from thinking to forming mental images in their mind about what they want, those thoughts become so powerful that nothing can stop the manifestation. If you don't like the images or mental pictures that have been formed in your mind, discard them, otherwise they will find expression in the physical world. For those mental pictures in your mind are powerful.

IF YOU MUST SUCCEED, BELIEVE IN YOUR IDEAS AND DREAM

FAITH
...according to your faith, be it unto you.
Matthew 9:29

What is oblivious to many people, is that they have no idea of the potency of faith or their belief system to bring to pass the desires of their heart. Again, it's not whether people believe in something or not; everyone believes in something, but the question is, 'What do you believe in?' Life and destiny is unto everyone according to your faith.

Believe you can and you're halfway there
-Theodore Roosevelt

If you believe you can, you probably can. If you believe you won't, you most assuredly won't. Belief is the ignition switch that gets you off the launching pad.
Dennis Waitley

If you believe you can or you believe you can't, either way you are probably right. So, please be careful of what you dream, think and imagine about, because those things have power to become realities in the physical world. This is how many people have unconsciously designed and created a life that they never wanted. They never knew those wrong thoughts and imaginations have power to replicate themselves in the physical world, thereby creating the circumstances and conditions of their lives. It's time to start changing your circumstances and conditions of life that you don't like, by changing the predominant thoughts and imaginations in your heart. So, we all forge our lives and shape the conditions of our lives with our thoughts, words, dreams and imaginations.

Your heart is the womb of your life and destiny, that is where your life and future is formed, that is where everything happens and takes place.

THE WOMB OF LIFE

I have observed that those five forces that shape life and destiny can be found in the heart, though some people interchangeably call it the mind. Those forces are found in the heart of each individual. Your heart is the womb of your life and destiny, that is where your life and future is formed, that is where everything happens and takes place. Whatever goes on in your heart will eventually find expression in the physical world. Just like a child is conceived in the womb of a woman, so is your life and destiny shaped in the womb of your heart.

For instance, when a woman meets with a man and there is fertilisation of her eggs, a baby begins to form in the womb and the gestation period is usually nine months. Most times, it takes about two weeks for the pregnancy to take place; depending on the nature of the body of the woman, sometimes they wouldn't even know they are pregnant. I have seen a woman who was pregnant but never knew until the sixth month. There are some women that get to know in the first month, some in the second month, or even third month, depending on their body. In all these cases, people might not even know that a woman is pregnant, even when they see her in public; she reveals to them that she is pregnant only when the pregnancy has become so conspicuous that everyone can see it. But one thing is certain, the sexual intercourse that led to the conception has set a gestation period of nine months in motion, during which the child is expected to fully develop before delivery takes place.

In the same way, whatever thoughts, ideas, imaginations or dreams that you conceive in your heart consciously or unconsciously, they automatically activate a gestation period during which they are expected to fully develop before they are delivered or manifested in the physical world. It's the nature of the thoughts of one's heart that give birth to their circumstances; so negative thoughts and imaginations also birth undesirable circumstances and conditions of life. We create our circumstances by the constant thoughts and imaginations of our heart. Your thoughts eventually become words and lead to action; every thought or idea or imagination you sustain long enough in your heart will eventually manifest when its gestation period is accomplished.

The delicate thing about this is that we don't know the gestation periods of our thought and imaginations; some may take a few weeks, some may take months, while others could take years to develop and then manifest. It doesn't matter the gestation period, as they will always manifest. Because we don't have control over the gestation periods of our thoughts and imaginations, the Bible warns us about the state of our heart, and admonishes us to be careful of what we think about, because our thoughts will always manifest and become a reality whether we like it or not. So, the best thing we can do is to control the quality and nature of our thoughts, as we cannot determine the gestation period.

Keep thy heart with all diligence; for out of it are the issues of life.

Proverbs 4:23

A good man out of the good treasure of the heart bringeth forth good things; and an evil man out of the evil treasure bringeth forth evil things.

Matthew 12:35

CREATE A COMPELLING DREAM

Dreamers are the greatest change agents in every generation. No generation can be changed without the emergence of dreamers. Dreamers hold the keys to the future, dreamers control the outcome of the future, dreamers are the hopes of every generation, dreamers give directions to their generation, and the direction of every generation is controlled by those who dare to dream.

Dreaming big is an attitude of those who believe in themselves. Everyone who truly believes in himself will always dare to dream big, because dreaming big is the secret of greatness. In order for depressed people to overcome depression and constant demoralisation, they have to dream and keep dreaming – and not just dreaming, but dreaming BIG dreams.

Creating a compelling dream keeps a man or a woman active and always energised to excel in life. Without dreams, life will be boring; when people complain of boredom, it is obvious that they either don't dream at all or don't know how to dream big, because dreaming big or compelling dreams usually instils joy and passion in the heart and keeps one energised, active and strong until the attainment of the dream. In any nation where there is constant depression and suicide cases, it is proof that the people are no longer dreaming big again.

Every civilisation was fashioned by dreamers, every technological advancement in any generation was set in motion by dreamers, every improvement and progress in any area of life was made possible by dreamers. Only dreamers can drive the desired changes in the world, and only dreamers can determine the destination of a nation. People can only grow from one level of progress to another, from one level of success to another, and from one level of greatness to another, by cultivating the habit of constantly dreaming big and compelling dreams.

BELIEVE YOU HAVE WHAT IT TAKES TO ACCOMPLISH IT

Most people fail to pursue their dream to the point of its actualisation because of self-doubt, which makes them think and believe they don't have what it takes to fulfil their dreams and live the quality of life they desire for themselves and become the kind of person they have always imagined to be. If you are ever going to achieve your dream, you must

IF YOU MUST SUCCEED, BELIEVE IN YOUR IDEAS AND DREAM

first believe that you have all it takes to achieve it; you must believe the resources are within your reach, and that all the things you will ever require will fall into place once you step out. Believing you have what it takes will make you defeat your self-doubts and self-imposed boundaries and limitations, and you will see yourself rising above your fears and reaching unto your dream.

Faith gives power; it doesn't necessarily make it easy, but it will make it possible. A lot of people are trapped in the wrong and negative self-debilitating thoughts, believing that they need to be something special before they can achieve their dreams. They feel that they are not qualified and empowered to achieve their goals in life, and the reason is because they have been looking at and thinking about the wrong things. Everything is within you, everything you will ever need is not outside, but right within you.

YOU ARE A SEED; PLANT YOURSELF

You are like a seed. God created everyone to be like a seed, and if you understand the nature of the seed, you will realise you have everything inside of you. Within a seed is its root, stem, branches, leaves and fruit; none of these comes from outside.

'Success is the by-product of right decisions and actions'

Everything is embedded within it; all that is required of the seed is to be planted in the right environment and soil. If you plant a seed in the right soil and environment, leave it and come back to it in few months or years, you will see a mighty tree, with its trunk, stem and fruit, flourishing without anyone's support. Just like when a child is born, as little the child is, it has the complete features of a full-grown man or woman, but you may not see them right away because he or she is still a child. There is no difference between a girl born now and a mature woman who has all her features fully developed. The only difference is time, and perhaps food. Feed the girl appropriately and, years to come, she will have all her own feminine features fully developed because everything was factored into her when she was created.

God didn't create anything incomplete; He didn't create you incomplete, either. God is smart enough not to create a seed and expect the external environment to give it root, or branches or its fruits. God couldn't have created us incomplete so that, as one grows, he or she will have to go and beg another person to complete the missing parts. God knows man is wicked, that if we were to depend on people to be complete, God knows many people will be happy to see others incomplete. All you need is to plant yourself in the right environment and in the right soil, like a seed, and forget about the rest; you will naturally excel if you do the right thing. Actually, success is a by-product of right decisions and actions. It is not something you should pursue; if you make the right decisions and take the right action, you won't have to bother about being successful and accomplishing your dream and purpose.

Making the right decision is synonymous to planting a seed in the right soil or environment; while taking actions is like watering and weeding the seed. If you do this, there is nothing that can stop the seed from germinating and flourishing properly; it wouldn't need anyone to help it produce it fruits in its season. If you behave and act like a seed, patterning your life with the process a seed goes through, you will excel and accomplish all your dreams. Everything you need to excel is within you. If believe you have all it takes to rise to an unstoppable height in life, then you will.

BELIEVE IN SUCCESS

There is no need to pursue an idea or dream that you don't believe in. If you don't believe in success, or that you will excel against all odds, you will never achieve anything. Believe you will succeed, believe you can and believe nothing can stop you. Even if there is no reason to believe you can succeed, just believing you will succeed is enough.

IF YOU MUST SUCCEED, BELIEVE IN YOUR IDEAS AND DREAM

How much do you believe in success? Some people remain where they are and never make progress because they believe they have no part to play in their success. A lot of people have said to me that they don't believe they have to do anything to succeed, that God has already determined those who will succeed and those who will fail. That, if God hasn't designed or determined that you will succeed, then there is nothing you can ever do to change that.

That is a lie, because every man is the captain of their destiny. We have a choice! You have a choice in what you will eventually become in life. If you refuse to make a decision to succeed, you have already made a decision not to succeed, because not making a decision is also a decision and you must face the consequences. Like in one of my books, *Against All Odds*, I explained that if you leave a piece of land for a year or more and never plant anything on it, when you return you will notice that something has grown on it. It will most likely be weeds – what you don't like. I have seen a lot of people argue passionately and unyielding that 'what is going to happen is what will happen', but that is a lie. They leave their lives to chance because they believe what is going to happen is what will happen, what God has said is what will happen is what will happen. Well, for that to even happen, you still have a role to play to see what God said will happen to happen.

I stumbled on this story in the Bible and I was shocked and dumfounded. It is the story of Cain and Abel. Cain killed his brother Abel and God laid a curse on Cain. Cain cried to God telling Him that the curse was too heavy for him to bear, and that if any man sees him, they will kill him. In response to his cries, God put a mark on Cain so that no one would kill him if they saw him, and if that ever happened, there would be a seven-times vengeance upon anyone that killed him. In other words, it was a mark of preservation from death, so that Cain wouldn't be killed by any man in order for him to suffer for the consequences of his sins. However, some years after that encounter with God, Cain was killed by Lamech, one of his great grandchildren in the fifth generation. This is the account:

Behold, thou driven hast driven out this day from the face of the earth; and from thy face shall I be hid; and I shall be a fugitive and a vagabond in the earth; and it shall come to pass, that everyone that findeth me shall slay me.
And the LORD said unto him, therefore whosoever slayeth Cain, vengeance shall be taken on him sevenfold. And the LORD set a mark upon Cain, lest any finding him should kill him.
And La'mech said unto his wives, A'dah and Zil'lah, Hear my voice; ye wives of La'mech, hearken unto my speech: for I have slain a man [Cain] to my wounding, and a young man [Cain] to my hurt.
If Cain shall be avenged sevenfold, truly La'mech seventy and sevenfold.
Genesis 4:14-15,23-24

Then I began to ask and wonder, was this not a man with a mark of preservation and command from God that no one would kill him, what happened? However, the attitude of the Lamech that killed him revealed a crucial important point and proved the truth that you have a part to play to achieve your dreams; it's not totally dependent on God what each individual will become on Earth. Cain didn't take personal responsibility to enforce the prophecy over him; however, when he was killed, the man that killed him established a prophecy on his own life, saying that he himself shall be avenged seventy-sevenfold should anyone kill him, and he made it known to his wife.

It became very obvious that greater responsibility rests on every individual to determine the outcome of his or her life. Even Cain had enough sense to tell God that the punishment was too much for him to bear, that he had to interfere with God's decision and God reduced it. Friends, so much depends on you if you really desire to fulfil your dream and be outstanding in life. My big brother, Chijioke Okonkwo, once told me this shortly before I left for the UK, the very last day I was with him, that, **'You can change any prophecy from anyone that you don't like.'** He made me understand that there is a realm you get to in the realm of the spirit, where you can change negative prophecies, or any prophecy at all, that you don't like; that, in such realm, even witches will leave you alone because they know you are far beyond their realm. This is why everyone, especially believers in Christ Jesus, should journey deeper into the spiritual; for the spiritual sphere is an infinite realm and we are to journey deeper into it in our personal walk with God, otherwise you will live an ordinary life.

PURSUING YOUR IDEAS AND DREAMS
'If at first the idea is not absurd, then there is no hope for it.'

Albert Einstein

The first step in the pursuit and actualisation of your dream is having unwavering and unyielding faith and confidence in the reality of your dream, for without faith nothing can be possible. Faith is the key that turns the handle of impossibility to possibilities; faith is the key do the actualisation of your dreams; faith is the power that makes the impossible possible. However, faith does not make your dream easy, but it makes it possible.

One major reason people don't pursue their idea is because it seems stupid and absurd when they first conceived or thought about it, but it was Albert Einstein that said, 'If at first the idea is not absurd, then there is no hope for it.' Most people's ideas seemed far more absurd than yours, yet they still pursued after their ideas and succeeded. You have to give life to your ideas and dreams by believing in yourself,

> *'Many people fail in life not for lack of big dreams, but because they failed to pursue and commit to their dreams'*

in your potentials, that you have all it takes to succeed, and that you will succeed, and then you must pursue your dream because that is the only factor that can make it a reality.

Many people still think that there are impossibilities, but if you have followed through the writings in this book, you will have understood that there is nothing like impossibility, because impossibility is dependent on human factors. Faith is a supernatural force and there is nothing supernatural that can be limited and stopped by the physical elements in the universe.

Without believing in yourself and in your dreams, you can never accomplish anything significant in life. Without faith in the credibility and authenticity of your dream, you can never turn your dreams into reality. So, the first step towards the fulfilment of your dream is having an unwavering and unshakable faith and confidence in the authenticity and reality of your dream.

It's not just enough to dream big, compelling dreams, but you have to believe in the dream, and the proof of your belief in your dream is your pursuit of the dream. Many people fail in life not because they don't have a dream, but because they failed to pursue their dreams. Without pursuit and commitments to your dreams, they can never see the light of the day, for it is the pursuit and commitment that turns your dream into reality.

> *'It's not the magnitude of an idea that makes it great, but your pursuit and commitment to the success of the idea'*

Most often, the difference between achievers and non-achievers doesn't lie in the scope of their talents or size of their dreams, but most of all the extent and degree of their commitment and pursuit of their dreams. Many people

IF YOU MUST SUCCEED, BELIEVE IN YOUR IDEAS AND DREAM

think that just having a big idea is what makes it great and determines the success of it, but that is not true because what gives an idea life is your pursuit and commitment to it. Without your pursuit and commitment to an idea, it will be lifeless and never come to fruition. Little things done in an extraordinary manner is what makes things great and extraordinary.

No one was really born great, we all achieve greatness in life by doing little things in great ways, and we become extraordinary by doing ordinary things in an extraordinary way. Understand that it's not the type of profession or career you are in that determines your success in that career or profession, but what you choose to do with it; what you decide to make out of it is what determines the level of your success. So, a medical doctor doesn't become successful and great simply because he is a medical doctor; an engineer will not become successful simply because he is an engineer; a footballer will never become successful simply because he decided to become a footballer or sportsman; a pastor will never become successful simply because he is a pastor; and an entrepreneur or businessman will not become successful simply because being an entrepreneur is lucrative. If you carefully look around you, you will probably realise that there are poor medical doctors around you; unsuccessful sportsmen around you; poor engineers around you; and, of course, poor business people or entrepreneurs around you.

> *No one was really born great, we all achieve greatness in life by doing little things in great ways, and we become extraordinary by doing ordinary things in an extraordinary way.*

Conversely, if you also do some research, you will find that there are very successful doctors in the world like Ben Carson; you will also notice there are super-successful and legendary footballers and sportsmen in the world like Cristiano Ronaldo and Lionel Messi; you will also learn that there are great engineers and successful businesspeople and entrepreneurs around you. The reason is that profession or career doesn't make people rich or wealthy but what they do with their profession or career.

A footballer or musician who practises for long hours daily will definitely be greater than the one who practises just for an hour or less a day; a business person who works diligently and more hours daily will definitely be greater than the one who is lazy; and a student who reads more and stays up late at night studying will definitely get a better result than the one who sleeps all nights. That is the principle by which the universe is designed – the principle of 'Cause and Effect'.

'Life was designed to be predicted by the things we do daily and consistently; you can't get out of life more than what you are willing to put into it'

You can't get out of life more than what you are willing to put into life. Life was designed to be predicted by the things we do daily and consistently; you can't alter the design of the universe. The world operates by principles and, in order to succeed, you must discover the governing principle around the endeavour or area of life for which you seek success and excellence. However, the common denominators of success in all aspects of life are discipline, diligence, determination, hard work, commitment, persistence and consistence. These are the primary common ratios of success in every aspect of life where you seek success and excellence.

'All the adversity I've had in my life, all my troubles and obstacles, have strengthened me… You may not realize it when it happens, but a kick in the teeth may be the best thing in the world for you.'
–Walt Disney

CHAPTER TEN
PUT YOUR DREAM TO THE TEST

'The price of achieving your dream is sacrifice'

The price of achieving your dream is sacrifice. Sacrifice is the price of victory and greatness in life, as no one can achieve anything meaningful in life without adequate sacrifice for it. Sacrifice is the supreme evidence of what you believe to be true and are convinced about. If you truly believe in your future and in destiny, then you must be willing to pay the sacrifice to fulfil it. Nothing great comes easy or is offered to you on a platter of gold; most often, the level of sacrifice required to fulfil a purpose determines the worth of the goal. Don't follow a path that has no obstacles because it will not lead you into greatness.

The path of greatness is paved with the stones of rejection, criticisms, hatred, and all kinds of oppositions you can't imagine. The price of achieving your dream is sacrifice; and if you are pursuing any dream that doesn't require you to make a huge sacrifice, or change either your sleeping time, eating and spending habits, then don't bother about it, because it wouldn't lead you to anything meaningful in life. According to John C. Maxwell, facing criticism is one of the prices you have to pay to achieve your dream.

If you truly believe in yourself and in your dream, then prove it and put it to the test by stepping out of your comfort zone to make the necessary sacrifice to achieve it. Most of the time, the difference between losers and winners is just the extra effort they had to put in to see their dream manifest, the resilience to hang in there when the going gets tough. Things will always go awry and contrary to your expectations, you will always encounter oppositions and challenges that stand in the way of your dream actualisation, but what matters is your ability to keep pushing till you achieve your goals.

YOUR TRUE IDENTITY

Your true Identity (ID) is defined as = your I(Idea) + your D(Dream). Your real identity is what you are known for. What is your idea and the dream you brought to light? What will you be known for? What contribution are you making for your generation? What is your contribution to making the world a better place, that the future generation will remember you for? Your real identity is not your physical look, because there will always be so many people that look exactly like you. There are twins that are so identical to the point that people can't differentiate between them. I have seen so many people that look exactly like me; in fact, one day I was walking along and a young man ran towards me shouting 'John, John, John!' Upon touching my sleeve, he realised I wasn't John, and he pleaded with me for forgiveness as I looked and walked exactly like someone he knew as John.

That was in my secondary school and I was told the same by most people. Sometimes, we even find people who bear the same names. Therefore, our true identity is not our names and physical looks, but our ideas and dreams that have contributed to make the world a better place. When we talk about the Wright Brothers, you remember the aeroplane; when we talk automobiles, we remember Henry Ford; when we talk about computers, you remember Bill Gates; when you talk about Facebook, you remember Mark Zuckerberg; when you talk about South Africa Independence, you remember Nelson Mandela; when we talk about racial equality, you remember Martin Luther King Jnr; when we talk about the Greatness of the Great Britain, especially during World War Two, you remember Winston Churchill; when we talk about electricity, you remember Michael Faraday; when we talk about the electric bulb, you remember Thomas Edison. So, what will the world remember you for? Your real identity is your idea and dream that blessed the lives of people; it may not be known all around the world, but it should be felt by the people around you.

PERSISTENCE IN THE FACE OF REJECTION
'Those who have cultivated the habit of persistence seem to enjoy insurance against failure. No matter how many times they are defeated, they finally arrive up toward the top of the ladder.'
Napoleon Hill

One of the concrete signs that you truly believe in yourself and in the reality of your ideas and dreams is your ability to persist even in the face of limitations, oppositions and obstacles of life. If you truly believe in yourself and in your capability to excel, you will prove it by your ability to persist even in the face of contrary evidences. Life is full of oppositions and challenges, and on the way to achieving your dreams you will eventually encounter misfortunes and different kinds of oppositions, but only those who truly believe in themselves will persevere and persist until they have attained their goals. Giving up too quickly is a strong sign that you don't truly believe in your ideas and in your dreams; it implies that you have a very weak desire and don't know the reason why you truly desire to be successful in life. You don't necessarily have to have plenty of reasons for your desire in order to fulfil it; just having one strong, convincing, concrete reason is enough to pull you through all the challenges and obstacles until you achieve your dreams and desires.

Persistence is actually a quality of one's character and this is usually derived from one's belief and confidence in himself and in his dreams and ideas. What you truly believe in, you will be willing to pursue and make the necessary sacrifices until you see its attainments. Many people give up and quit in the face of the first sign of defeat or misfortune; that symbolises weak desire or lack of faith in one's self and dreams. If you truly believe in yourself and in your dreams, you will not easily give up; you will not throw in the towel.

No matter what you face, you will always hang in there until you have achieved your dreams and desire; it is a quality of champions to see to the end, to hang in there until victory is achieved. Winners don't quit too early. The difference between champions and losers is not necessarily talent or skill, but more often than not it has to do with the quality of persistence, of being able to see the finish line and persevere long enough until they get to the finish line of their race and dreams.

Endurance is a great quality for athletes who must finish their race. The quality of being able to persevere until you get to the finish line most times is the distinguishing feature and major determinant of success in life. It is the hallmark of victors and conquerors in life, because they understand that there will always be oppositions, obstacles, criticisms and rejections, but in the midst of all these, they are resolute and determined to persevere until they attain their desires and see their dreams turned into reality.

Giving up too soon, especially at the first sign of defeat, failure, opposition, limitation, rejection or criticism, is actually a sign of lack of confidence and belief in one's self and one's dreams. It is a major test of your faith in yourself. If you have faith and strong conviction in yourself and in your dream, you will be able to follow through to the end until you see the manifestation of that which you desire.

SUCCEEDING IN SPITE OF REJECTIONS

Some of the inspiring stories of people whose ideas and dreams were vehemently rejected and criticised before they succeeded were that of J.K Rowling and Walt Disney. They suffered strong rejections but, in the midst of all that, they didn't give up on their dreams and ideas because they had strong beliefs and convictions in themselves and their ideas and dreams; that was why I defined one's real identity as the combination of their ideas and dreams. When we talk about Harry Potter, you remember J.K Rowling, when we talk about Disneyland, Walt Disney World, animated cartoon films, and cartoon characters like Mickey Mouse, you remember Walt Disney, to mention but a few people. That is their identities, what they were known for. There may be other persons bearing the same names as theirs, but what distinguishes them are their ideas and dreams that were turned into reality. You will not be identified by what you wished and hoped for, but by what you accomplished.

J.K. ROWLING AND THE FAMOUS HARRY POTTER SERIES

In attempt to turn her ideas and dream into reality, J.K. Rowling was rejected and turned down twelve times by publishers who told her that her book was not good enough and wouldn't have any market value. She had taken years, in spite of all the odds to write the famous Harry Potter story, but publishers were not willing to publish her book because they said it would be a waste of resources, energy and time to publish such a book written by a woman, but J.K. Rowling wouldn't give up on herself and on her ideas and dream. She believed in herself first, and then in the power of her ideas and dream; and her commitment and persistence to follow through to the end proved that persistence is a major force that turns the hand of failure and rejection to success and victory.

The story of the life J.K. Rowling is quite an inspiring one, especially for the young people of the present and future generation. The life she leads today is so different from the one she led in the 1990s, such that even her name has changed. Popularly known across the world as J.K. Rowling, but unknown to most people is the fact that her middle initial is not included in her legal name. When she went to a publisher to publish her novel, the publisher told her that young boys might not be willing to read a book written by a woman and that she should use initials instead. Having just the letter 'J' in her name, she created a middle name for herself, Kathleen, after her grandmother.

Several years later, she might be certain to justify what prompted the idea for Harry Potter. She was on transit on a train from Manchester to London when she conceived the idea to write the book. The ideas saturated her mind until she got to her destination, to the extent that she was so excited and filled with joy at the thought of writing the book, as she stated in her interview with Oprah Winfrey in 2010. Unfortunately for her, she had to pass through many challenges and problems such as her mother's death, her divorce, as well as financial constraints. After her divorce, she had to begin life afresh as a single mother with lots of financial pressures; she couldn't even afford to pay for her rent, yet she didn't give up on her ideas. For people who truly believe in themselves and in their ideas, there is no challenge and obstacle of life that is strong enough to discourage them and make them give up on their ideas; they usually fight through to the end until they have achieved their dream. They fight for their dream, they never let it go!

After the painstaking effort of finally completing her book, she needed someone to publish the book for her and she went in search of publishers. She wrote to several of them, but she was met with stark rejection. If you go to her Twitter handle, you will see one of the rejection letters sent to her from one of the publishers who declined her request, which had been uploaded there at the request of one her fans.

Rowling strongly believed in her ideas and what she had to offer. She was sure, beyond a shadow of a doubt, that her book was worth reading and would add value to anyone who read it, despite what the publishers said. She never allowed their negative opinions and criticisms to stop her or lose faith, either in herself or in her dream and ideas. Actually, if people can easily confuse you and make you lose faith in yourself and ideas, then you don't truly know and believe yourself. To excel in life, one must develop unyielding, uncompromising and unshakable confidence and faith in one's self and capability to succeed.

It doesn't take many talents and gifts to excel; it takes much more faith and confidence in one's self and ideas and dreams. J.K. Rowling kept her faith and hopes alive. She didn't allow her ideas and dreams to drown in the rivers and oceans of publishers' rejections and negative criticisms; she didn't bury her faith in herself and her ideas and dreams in the graveyard of financial scarcity and rejections. Instead, she fought her way to the top, and her dream kept her going until she finally met with success. That was the greatest test of her dream. Your ideas and dreams will be tested by life in the same way, to see if you truly believe in what you want to sell to the world; and, when the tests of life come, I hope you will not easily give up and quit the race of success!

It took the thirteenth attempt for Rowling's book to be published. Like I said earlier in this book, destiny pays and, when it pays, it pays you bigger and better than anything else; that is why it's worth fighting for. Your ideas and dreams are worth fighting for if you truly believe in them. How was she able to manage the cascade of rejections? Some people would have given up even at the first sign of defeat and rejection, but not J.K. Rowling. Most people fail, not because of bad ideas and strategies, but for lack of persistence and resilience in the face of obstacles and oppositions. If some people had hung in there a little longer when the going got tough, they might have been very successful. Most failures and defeats in life are traceable to lack of resilience and persistence than lack of good ideas, gifts, and talents. This is why I always remember the words of Chijioke Okonkwo, 'Keep pushing.'

Overnight, Rowling was catapulted from her small apartment in Edinburgh to worldwide recognition. When destiny pays you, it will look as if you never suffered in the past, because it will pay you such that your many years of struggles and hardship will seem insignificant and irrelevant compared to the fortune, success and greatness it will bring you. That is why most people don't know about the struggles and failures of great people unless they are told. When destiny pays you back for all your efforts, struggles, pains, patience, sacrifices and persistence, it will look like an overnight success, as if you have never suffered in your life. Give it all it takes, fight for your ideas and dreams, that is where your identity in the world lies. The world will remember you for the challenges you faced, but will pay you for your ideas and dreams you fulfilled.

When destiny pays you for your sacrifice and patience, you will forget all the years of struggles, labour and hardship. Today, Rowling's Harry Potter franchise is worth $7.7 billion. Reports say that she is richer than the Queen of England, but that wasn't the way it used to be. She was a single mother who depended on welfare, and her manuscripts were turned down and vehemently rejected by at least twelve publishers. Her story is an inspiring one and a motivation for anyone who is facing rejections and challenges in life. Her life proves what the Bible says, that the righteous fall seven times and still rise again. Believe me, even if you fail twenty times, you can rise twenty-one times if you don't give up on yourself and quit.

Source: [JK Rowling Turned Down By 12 Publishers Before Finding Success With Harry Potter Books (riseupeight.org)](#)

TALENT IS NEVER ENOUGH

Talent is never enough to make one successful; having ideas is not the only thing that makes one excel. I have seen so many people who are very skilled and talented, but are unsuccessful and mediocre, and so many of them put the blame on several factors except themselves. They are caught in the blame game web. It seems to me that there are more successful people with little talents and gifts but with persistence, than there are talented people who are unsuccessful. If talented and gifted people could be more persistent, I believe they would be super geniuses.

Cristiano Ronaldo of Portugal is one athlete who I know to be very persistent. He hardly quits. You can see that in his career, and that is probably one major quality that has distinguished him. He is not so skilful a dribbler as many other players like the Brazilian Garrincha, the Argentine legend Diego Maradona, the Nigerian legend Austin Jay-Jay Okocha, the great legend Pele, Zinedine Zidane, Lionel Messi, and the Brazilian Neymar Jnr. On the list of the top ten greatest dribblers in the world, he ranks tenth. However, one quality distinguishes him from all the talented and skilful players, both from the past and present contemporary, Lionel Messi, and that quality is persistence. His persistence was most evident when he won the 2016 European Championship for his country Portugal. (The top 10 greatest dribblers in world football history (No 7 is an African) - Opera News)

'Nothing in this world can take the place of persistence. Talent will not: nothing is more common than unsuccessful men with talent. Genius will not; unrewarded genius is almost a proverb. Education will not: the world is full of educated derelicts. Persistence and determination alone are omnipotent.'

Calvin Coolidge

WALT DISNEY REJECTED 300 TIMES
'All the adversity I've had in my life, all my troubles and obstacles, have strengthened me... You may not realize it when it happens, but a kick in the teeth may be the best thing in the world for you.'

Walt Disney

The story of Walt Disney is another story that proves persistence is a major quality that determines whether one will succeeds or not. There are more people with talents and gifts who are failures than there are persistent people with little talents and gifts. Most times, I wonder why some people with talents and gifts aren't doing so well compared to those who are not so gifted, but the reason is because persistence is an irreplaceable and indispensable quality in the equation of greatness; most great things in life were accomplished through persistence and resilience. It doesn't matter how great one's ideas and dreams are, without persistence to follow through to the end, there will never be success.

Sadly, Walt Disney is no longer with us but his impact and legacy live on, and his ideas and dreams will continue to shape the world and the generations to come. I am quite certain that people, including me, didn't know the ordeals he went through, the rejections he experienced and the obstacles he had to face to turn his dreams and ideas into reality. I did some research on his biography and discovered that he was rejected 300 times before his ideas and dream became a reality. When he conceived the idea for Mickey Mouse, Walt Disney was rejected by bankers 300 times because they thought the idea was absurd and wouldn't be successful. But, oblivious to them were the words of Albert Einstein, 'If at first the idea is not absurd, then there is no hope for it.'

The same idea the bankers thought was absurd and refused to fund, is now worth one billion US dollars today. If you are easily discouraged and depressed by people's negative opinions and comments about you, you probably won't go far in life; people will always have their own opinion, and it's normal for some people to discourage others and criticise them, but you wouldn't want to be their victim. The first thing is to understand that your ideas and dream will not be accepted by so many people, including those you trust and believe that they will always back you up. Understanding that anybody can reject you and your ideas will make you steadfast, unshakable and unmoveable in the face of rejection and discouragement. It's normal to be rejected and refused by others, but it's abnormal for you to get discouraged and give up because people rejected your ideas. It just proves you are not ready or prepared to succeed.

In fact, rejection is a welcome pack for you in your journey of success. It is the first and compulsory test of your ideas and dream if you truly believe in yourself and your ideas and dream. Anyone who passes this test with an 'A' will most likely succeed against all the odds; but if you fail this simple first test, you will inevitably crash out of the brace of success and championship.

Had Walt Disney given up on his ideas and dream anywhere between the 2nd to 299th rejection, the world would never have known about his creativity such as *Aladdin*, *The Lion King* or *Beauty & The Beast*. These classics were impactful such that almost every home in the world had the cartoon classics, and every child in the world wanted to watch them. I don't think I can imagine what it was like for him to be rejected over 250 times, because I haven't been rejected that many times, even though I have experienced rejection in sales as a marketer. It might be easy to overcome a few rejections and still make your sales, but I wouldn't know what it was like for him to have been turned down three hundred times.

> *'Most times, what people need is not more talents, gifts, and great ideas, but more convictions, perseverance, persistence and self-belief.'*

However, it proves to every one of us that there is actually nothing like impossibility. Our possibility level is determined by the degree of our success-belief drive, the extent to which one is willing to endure and go until they hit the success-belief threshold – the measure of faith that no amount of rejection, obstacles, and opposition can quench until success is achieved. Indeed, possibility or impossibility is competence-based, persistence-based, perseverance-based, knowledge-based, and information-based.

Nothing in itself is actually impossible, but our attitude towards a particular objective is what either makes it possible or impossible, and therefore determines whether we can achieve our dreams or not. Most times, what people need is not more talents, gifts, or great ideas, but more perseverance, persistence and self-belief. We need more self-belief than we need more talents; the talent you already have is enough, only if you will believe more in yourself. More self-belief is what most people need to succeed, not more connections or great ideas. It is interesting to know that Walt Disney was fired by a newspaper company he worked for because they said he lacked creativity, yet he went on to build the Walt Disney company some years later. So, what he needed wasn't more creativity or talents, because everything was already inside him when he was sacked.

'All the adversity I've had in my life, all my troubles and obstacles, have strengthened me... You may not realize it when it happens, but a kick in the teeth may be the best thing in the world for you.'
Walt Disney

Just like a seed, our future is already within us; what will make you is already within you; your genius is lying dormant within you, just waiting for the day you will awaken it. Your potentials, talents and gifts are all within you, waiting for to make a demand on them; they are sleeping inside of you, waiting for your wake-up call when you need them. I believe that when Walt Disney was sacked from his job, that was his own wake-up call to make him aware of the potentials and greatness that lay dormant within him. Sometimes, your misfortunes and problems are the wake-up calls for what lie within you. Those who are successful will understand this. Other people, had they been sacked, they wouldn't have the audacity to begin their own business and build a global empire.

Every adversity carries an equivalent seed of benefit; every adversity is pointing you to something useful that you haven't paid attention to. The greatness inside of you is craving for attention and expression and, in order to get the attention it deserves, sometimes it creates an unfortunate event or adversity for you, such as getting sacked from a job, illness, or even a relationship breakdown. It just means that you can come to a place of solitude and personal meditation and reflection, make amends, come up with better plans and strategies, and then see the opportunities you have been missing all your life.

'Every adversity, every failure, every heartbreak, carries with it the seed of an equal or greater benefit.' 'In every adversity lies the seed of an equal or greater opportunity.'
Napoleon Hill

For instance, in football, a team that may have been losing in the first half had a dramatic comeback in the second half because of the fifteen-minute break it had. In the UEFA Champions League, we have teams that lost to their opponents in the first leg, but in the second leg they were able to overturn the score and win. One such match was PSG and Barcelona in the 2017 Champions League round 16 of the first leg; PSG took the lead with four goals to nil, but in the second leg Barcelona turned the defeat around, which has never been done in the history of football, turning around a 4-0 defeat. Liverpool also turned around a 3-0 defeat to Barcelona in the 2019 semi-finals of the Champions League; they had conceded goals in the first leg, but went ahead to overturn the defeat in the second leg and eventually won the Champions League. Nigeria also had a historic event in the Atlanta Olympics in 1996, where they had to overturn a 3-1 defeat to Brazil and eventually won the gold medal.

It doesn't matter how absurd an idea is, being persistent enough can

'Nothing in itself is actually impossible, but our attitude towards our dreams and aspirations is what either makes it possible or impossible, and therefore determines whether we can achieve it or not.'

turn those absurd ideas into an outstanding success. The idea itself is nothing without other factors of success such as persistence and diligence, for these are the qualities that make one successful and great. We need more men and women who have convictions in themselves and in their ideas and dreams, than people of more talents and special gifts. We need more people with more self-belief and confidence in themselves than we need people with more talents and gifts.

'All the adversity I've had in my life, all my troubles and obstacles, have strengthened me… You may not realize it when it happens, but a kick in the teeth may be the best thing in the world for you.'

Walt Disney

Source: Walt Disney Was Fired & Rejected 300 Times - Failure To Success | Succeed Feed

'If the United States of America or Britain is having elections, they don't ask for observers from Africa or Asia, but when we have elections, they want observers.'
—Nelson Mandela

CHAPTER ELEVEN
AFRICA, WE MUST BELIEVE IN OURSELVES TO RISE

'Ask not what your country can do for you –
ask what you can do for your country.'
—John F. Kennedy

History tells us that Africa was the cradle of development and the centre of learning and excellence. Many other nations came to Africa to learn about the secret of its development. Unfortunately, Africa has lost the light and now it doesn't seem possible that Africa was once a leading nation. For instance, there was a time when the Nigerian Naira had greater value than the US dollar, but today the difference between the US dollar and Nigerian Naira is like the distance between the East and the West. I don't want to talk about the problems that Africa is experiencing, as it's so obvious that the blind can see it, and many people have written about it and I don't want to write more on that subject.

From my own perspective, if Africa is to rise again and take her place among the industrialised nations of the world, then one thing is for sure: we have to believe in ourselves. Africa must believe in her own ability to rise without having to depend on the Western world for anything. At the root of all the problems of Africa is a lack of belief in ourselves and in our ability and capacity to lift the continent from poverty and backwardness.

The plague that has befallen Africa is lack of belief in ourselves. This is the major pandemic that has plagued Africa and it's worse than either cancer or the coronavirus disease. Until Africa sets herself loose from the mental slavery, bondage and captivity that makes its people think like slaves, who have been disadvantaged in every respect, we can never rise and take our place among great nations. The solution to the African problem is not in the hands of the government of other strong nations; Africa must arise again and discover where and when the rain of adversity, corruption, poverty, and backwardness began to beat down on her in order to dry her body of this evil rain.

Africa is full of endless potentials and possibilities, but they can only be actualised and maximised if we can believe in ourselves and what we are capable of achieving. Thinking that the solution is in the hands of the UK or USA is a slavery mindset which will only keep the continent in perpetual darkness, captivity and bondage. Every nation and continent is peculiar and their respective competitive advantages are quite peculiar to each. For instance, the kind of weather that characterises a nation is suitable to its nature and everything it produces is with reference to the climate it experiences. The people from those nations are different physically from that of the blacks, and therefore will require a different maintenance culture. For instance, when Covid-19 hit the world, Nigeria and Africa were the least affected because of the scourging sun and heat that is prevalent there.

Every nation and continent has its peculiar advantages, so importing and adopting the techniques that work well in another continent and expecting them to work in our continent will be tantamount to putting a round peg in a square hole. We can't adopt the same style of constitution, political structure or system of government of another nation to solve our own problems and political mess. The USA got its independence from Great Britain, but their government has an entirely different kind of constitution and political structure. The USA practises the presidential system of government, while their colonial master practises the parliamentary system and the monarchy. There is even American English and British English, meaning that the USA didn't have to depend on and adopt everything from the British.

Every nation and continent is expected to evolve and keep

evolving; and, in the process, develop tactics and strategies that are consistent with their own nature and developmental prospect. The problems that Nigeria is experiencing are not about having too many ethnic groups, its population, religion, or too many tribes, but because it is trying to copy the Western method of development and government that is consistent with their peculiarity. Therefore, we Africans can't adopt such style. Our solutions lie within us and in our own hands; we must believe in ourselves and our special talents and abilities God has endowed us with.

WE MUST BELIEVE IN OUR INGENUITY

There is great creativity in Africa. Africa is blessed with so much creative ideas and potentials to do great things. Great things have been done in Africa, great men and women have risen from Africa, great leaders have emerged from Africa, great talents and potentials have developed from Africa. Therefore, we should not be inferior or termed as a third world. The term 'third world' is just someone's ideology, not a reality; Africa must rise up to prove the world wrong. There are many great people from Africa all over the world doing exceptionally well and leading world-class organisations, like Dr. Okonjo-Iweala, the Director-General of the World Trade Organization. There are many Africans in different parts of the world whose achievements and creativity have proven that creativity, greatness and success is not colour or race biased; rather, it's a universal phenomenon.

This is not a book to chronicle the great achievements and names of outstanding men and women from the continent of Africa, so we must believe that our solutions lie in us and in accepting and believing in whom we are, in our nation and race. I am not ashamed to be an African, because there is no other place like Africa. It's a beautiful place and I will always be proud of my origins. God didn't make any mistake by sending me to Africa, and we must all uphold and sustain this mindset so that we can rise and be great once again. Africa was once great, so where did we miss it? Where did the rain of poverty and backwardness start beating down on Africa?

It's time for us all to unite and rise again. In the words of Dr David O. Oyedepo, 'It doesn't have to be whites to be right.' We don't have to wait for the approval of the Western world before we can believe in ourselves and in what we can do, just as you don't have to wait for the approval of other people before you can feel good and believe in yourself. In the same way, Africa doesn't have to wait for the applause and approval of any other continent before we can believe in ourselves and accept our own creativity.

The greatest display of lack of belief in ourselves is shown in our consumer behaviour, where we refuse to eat what we produce, and import everything a white man produces because we believe that only the things made in UK or USA, or Turkey or Japan, or France are original and the best. We have to invest in ourselves. Our government should invest in indigenous industries and we must accept our own products, patronise ourselves, and where there are lapses we should improve and improvise to keep enhancing and improving until we get there.

I implore the governments of Abia and Anambra states to invest massively in Aba main market and Onitcha international markets, respectively. There are so many potentials and creative abilities in such places and, if harnessed, they should have been a centre of international attention and revenue generation. We must believe in ourselves. I have bought good-quality clothes in Aba market that have lasted for several years, which I would never have imagined. We have talents, we must believe in 'Made in Nigeria' or Africa. We must accept our own creativity, consume it and consistently improve all that we do. Greatness is not far from Africa; we only have to believe that we have all it takes to excel.

WE MUST STOP EXAGGERATING OUR PROBLEMS

There is no nation that doesn't have a challenge or problem. We can't expect the British government or American government to abandon their own problems to solve ours. Every nation is battling with one problem or the other. No nation is perfect. As great as the UK, USA, Germany, France and Canada are, they all have their own challenges and are striving hard to solve their problems. They love themselves, play down on their problems and celebrate their greatness and the vision they have set for their nations.

We must stop exaggerating our problems and start solving them; we must celebrate our talents, promote our achievements internationally. We must help one another and unite again to fight our common enemy. There is no nation that is free of problems and challenges; it's obvious the opportunities are more prevalent in the Western world, but it wasn't always like that. From time immemorial, they decided to make their nations and continents what they are today; they built themselves and created their own space; they desired greatness for their people and nation and, therefore, created the limitless opportunities that abound in their nations.

If we truly want to develop, we have to tell ourselves the truth and elect the right people into public offices and allow them to lead the nation freely. There are great minds in Nigeria. Whenever I look at Nigeria and remember the countless number of great minds and competent human resources that are capable of leading the nation from darkness into light, but are denied the opportunity to lead, I weep. The problem truly is within us, not in the hands of the Western world. We have qualified and competent, intelligent and smart people who are capable of transforming the nation and leading our nation into the promised land. We must allow the qualified and competent to rule; we must not allow tribalism, religious differences and corruption to distort our sense of reasoning. The solution is within us;

our messiah is in our boarders, the solutions we seek from the outside world are right within us. We have everything in us to rise.

WE ARE NOT INFERIOR TO ANY RACE

I write to every son and daughter of Africa in any part of the world to believe that they are not inferior to any race or continent, and that we must not allow ourselves to be intimidated or relegated to the position of a nonentity. We must accept our race and colour and believe in the limitless possibilities that lie within us. Small thinking, disadvantaged and slavery mindset are the major limitations to our destinies and potentials; we must believe in ourselves and accept who we are. That is the cure to an inferiority complex. You don't necessarily have to be competent to be confident; if you are confident in yourself, you will become competent in anything you do. Every limitation we face is the one we have acknowledged in our mind and accepted to be reality; for, eventually, everyone's belief will become their reality. It's what you believe that becomes your reality in life, so don't play the victim game and feel inadequate or disadvantaged in any way.

God didn't create any race to be inferior to another. If you ever feel inferior or think yourself to be inadequate and disadvantaged in any way, you have made yourself that way because greatness is an attitude. It's doing little things in an extraordinary way, doing little things excellently that makes you great and exceptional. Africa must liberate itself from the slavery and inadequate mindset in order to rise. This is a wake-up call to all the nations of the African continent to believe in themselves and stop looking to other nations for a solution and assistance. We can do it, we can rise and we can do great things. Let's arise to prove to the world we are not third world – or a second-class race, as they have assumed that is what Africa is. I see a new continent of Africa; I see a new Nigeria and I see a greater people emerging and rising from the continent of Africa. For we were created for greatness and greatness flows in our veins and arteries.

AFRICA IS NOT A REFUSE DUMP

Like I have said, the development of Nigeria and Africa doesn't lie in the hands of the West, but in our mindset. The starting place in our quest for growth and transformation of the nation of Nigeria, and Africa as a whole, is our mental liberation and emancipation from lack of belief and confidence in ourselves and potentials. Africa is greatly blessed, and most especially Nigeria. Nigeria has boundless mineral resources and also competent human capital needed to transform the nation from where it is today into an industrialised and developed nation of the world, and I believe there is no nation in the world that is as blessed and wealthy as Nigeria.

There is no nation in this world that has experienced and suffered the kind of looting and corruption as Nigeria, that would still be rich and wealthy as Nigeria is. Yet, Nigeria is still blessed with abundant resources. The root of the problem of our nation is a complete lack of belief in ourselves as a black nation. We trust the judgement of the Western world more than ours. We believe more in what they produce than what we produce.

We have crude oil, yet Nigeria exports crude oil to the UK and still imports the refined petroleum products from them because the Nigerian government doesn't believe that we can actually refine the crude oil by ourselves. There were times when there was bunkering in the nation, and they termed it illegal refining of crude oil; but that illegally refined crude oil was actually consumed in the Nigerian nation. If the government was wise, it would have seen the talents and potentials in those people and invested in the indigenous technology invented and adopted by them, to refine the crude oil in order to develop it for national use; but the government didn't, because it believes that the technology invented by the whites is better. So, we prefer the products from foreign nations to that of our own land because we don't believe in ourselves; we don't believe in what we can do; we don't believe the solution is in ourselves.

I feel deep pains to see how Nigerians abroad have turned the nation of Nigeria into a dumping ground. I was privileged to accompany my landlord, who is a Nigerian, to the storage arena where they usually load trucks with cargo they send to Nigeria, and I began to weep. For these were people who had been in Europe for over three decades and they were sending back 40-foot containers full of scraps. One of the men I met there shared his experience with me, that most of the cargo was scraps that were no longer useful. My fellow Nigerians saw it as a great business enterprise to buy them off cheaply and send to Nigeria.

My pain was I saw used mattresses, old beds, furniture, spoilt electronics, old plates and cups, used clothes and different items that have rusted away. I asked one of the men, 'Why are they sending these things to sell in Nigeria? Are there no carpenters in Nigeria to produce new beds? Or no wood in Nigeria to produce tables and chairs? Is all the cotton in Nigeria now so scarce such that they have to send bags of used clothes and materials to sell to people?' They believe that whatever is from the Europe, including scraps, is best quality and better than anything that can be produced in Nigeria.

We have carpenters in Nigeria, we have forests with inexhaustible quantities of trees that can be felled to produce furniture, so why are Nigerians abroad buying and sending scraps that are not useful in Europe to Nigeria to sell? The lack of belief in ourselves as Africans, and especially Nigerians, has made the nation of Nigeria and Africa itself a dumping ground for scraps in the name of the importation business! This must stop immediately! It's time to change the narrative and that begins with our mental emancipation and transformation, where we believe in ourselves and our potentials, that we are not inferior to any race or continent.

FINDING YOUR VOICE AS A BLACK RACE

'Change will not come if we wait for some other person or some other time. We are the ones we've been waiting for. We are the change that we seek.'
Barack Obama

Being black is not a reason to be backward in life

Being black is not a reason to be backward in life because the factors that make for outstanding accomplishments are not external qualities like race, gender, skin colour, appearance, body structure or height. It's a mental disorder and a misnomer to still think that one's colour or race offers an advantage to be successful in life. In this 21st century, the factors of success have changed because our present generation is a knowledge generation or information age, making those with ideas the kings and queens of this age.

In an information age or knowledge era such as our generation, ideas rule the world and those with good ideas and strategies to rightly execute their ideas and add values to people will always be the leaders of this generation. In a knowledge-based era, knowledge and information are the key to dominating and ruling the world; only ideas and strategies will win. You can't think of winning with the same rules and techniques that once triumphed and ruled in the past generations. During the medieval or dark ages, physical qualities counted for success and greatness then; they were relevant and indispensable in the past generations because of that age. However, in a knowledge and information age such as ours, it's an era of the 'triumph of ideas', a dispensation of the 'triumph of information', 'triumph and merchandise of knowledge'.

This is an era where the statement 'knowledge is power' is true. In this era, your height doesn't count, skin colour doesn't matter, your race becomes irrelevant and all the physical attributes and qualities that counted for success and greatness in the past centuries have become irrelevant in this dispensation. Therefore, thinking that race or the colour of one's skin is an advantage in this season is an illusion. In this era, the rules of the game of success have changed; in the medieval age, people were wealthy and great by the acres of land people had, alongside their physical strength to work hard.

The Four Historic Economic Revolutions

Since creation, man has experienced four major economic revolutions. The first economic revolution is known as the The Hunting Age, a period in humanity where nature provided the wealth. It was the period of hunting. During this age, socioeconomically, everyone was equal. The kings didn't have a higher standard of living than their subjects. This was an age when physical attributes and qualities such as height, body build or physical strength were an advantage and the keys to becoming influential and prosperous because those qualities enabled people to hunt.

Then, the world continued to revolve and got into the second economic revolution, which was The Agricultural Age. In this period, land became the source of wealth. It was a season of agricultural activities where people engaged in farming and also domesticated their animals. During this period, kings and queens owned the land, while their subjects worked on the land and paid taxes to the Royals. The kings rode horses while the peasants walked. Consequently, this created two socioeconomic classes: the rich and the peasants.

During this age, physical strength and agility were the keys because men needed to be physically strong and agile enough to farm; those who owned large acres of land ruled and dominated, and they were the employers of labourers who worked on their farms to earn their living. Those who had large acres of land married wives who were often equally as wealthy. This was the slave trade era, because slave masters needed men of strength to work on the land. It was in this age that the slave trade became very lucrative, as the slave masters needed them to work for them so as to produce wealth and become powerful. People's wealth was largely dependent on the number of slaves people had, the size of their land and the agricultural produce that their slaves produced. It was an era of manual labour and struggles.

It's very important to understand that, in both the hunting and agricultural ages, it was men who had the powers and ruled over the Earth. Women were subjects to men, because women didn't have the physical strength to either hunt or farm, so they primarily depended on their husbands or their labourers to provide the food and meet their needs. Their basic needs were food and shelter, so any man who was physically strong enough to hunt and farm, or owned lands for farming, were seen as responsible because they could provide for women. Therefore, women sought such men to marry as their husbands so their needs could be met.

The agricultural revolution then ushered in another economic revolution known as the Industrial Age. According to Robert T. Kiyosaki, the Industrial Age began in 1492, when Christopher Columbus and other explorers went in search of trade routes, lands, and resources. In this age, mineral resources like oil, copper, tin, rubber, etc, were the sources of wealth. In this period, industrial-use land was more valuable than agricultural lands. People began to make their wealth through the exploration of mineral deposits, especially oil. Many nations' economies became dependent on oil as their major source of revenue.

This led to the advent of three socioeconomic classes: the rich, the middle class, and the poor. This was the time during which industries and oil exploration became the major sources of wealth for people. It produced super-rich people like John D. Rockefeller, a major oil dealer who controlled and supplied almost 90 percent of the world's supply of oil, especially in the United States, where he was the major supplier of oil. He became the world's first billionaire.

Those who had industrial lands were the ones that

controlled wealth and were, therefore, highly successful. During this age, those with the technology explored the oil and other mineral resources, while those with the know-how had the advantage and controlled most of the wealth.

With the passage of time, this age heralded another crucial age, which is The Information Age. You can also call it the 'Idea or Knowledge' age because, in this era and dispensation, ideas and knowledge rule. The advent of this age brought equality to everyone. I refer to it as the 'equality age' as it provides a common ground and equal opportunity for anyone who can think and come up with useful ideas that can add value to humanity. I could call it the 'value age' because the worth of anyone in this dispensation depends on the value they can add to people and the society, and not their colour or race. This age displaces the advantages of the physical attributes and qualities of physical height, race and colour that counted for success in the previous ages. It enthroned character over colour, content over container, right over race, excellence over ethnicity. It enthroned knowledge and information as the king of the age, thereby making everyone on the Earth the master and captain of their fates, irrespective of their race, colour or gender.

This age began with the invention of digital computers. It's now technology and information that produces the wealth. In this information age, the price of becoming rich has become low, which means many people can get rich at low costs because information abounds everywhere and it's available for those that are interested. In this age, ideas rule the world. This age has created four socioeconomic classes of people: the poor, middle class, rich, and super-rich. Jeff Bezos is one of the most renowned of The Information Age super-rich.

This Information Age has opened the door to wealth and prosperity to both the male and female gender alike, and that is why we have wealthy billionaire women in the world today. This age doesn't recognise your religion or race, colour or gender, but your contribution to humanity. In the Information Age, anybody can make his or her wealth anywhere. It's no longer dependent on the colour or race, or the country you come from, but on your ideas and information. It is no longer important who you know (as they commonly say in Nigeria), but what you know. It becomes very easy to achieve more in less time.

There has never been a time in history where people are able to get wealth easier than this age, but many are still poor because they don't know the trend of economic revolutions, they don't know what age we are in now. They don't know that the rules of wealth have changed. They are still trying to operate in the 21st century with the rules of the past ages and dispensations.

Dispensation of Equal Opportunities

This Age of Information gives everyone equal access to opportunity, thereby making everyone responsible for the outcome of their lives and destiny, whether you are black or white, male or female; it doesn't count any more. It give us all equal rights and opportunities to prove our worth and show what stuff we are made of; it brings to light the beauty of competition and the triumph of excellence in our business world; it allows us all to remake and reinvent ourselves. It gives us all the opportunities to change the person that the world has made us, it give us the second, third and countless chances to keep improving ourselves and becoming better until we become the real person we dreamt of.

'Never underestimate the power of dreams and the influence of the human spirit. We are all the same in this notion: the potential for greatness lives within each of us.'
Wilma Rudolph

In the previous ages and dispensations, crippled people were seen as invalids who were useless and completely dependent on others for their welfare. In this new dispensation of enthronement and triumph of excellence, value-adding knowledge and ideas, the physically disabled can now become employers, employing those who are not physically challenged. The physically challenged can become highly successful, prosperous and great, just like Helen Keller, or Nick Vijudic the Australian preacher and author born without limbs or hands. It's because of this Information Age that we can have blind medical doctors, disabled pilots and different kinds of physically challenged people who are not sorry for themselves, because they know their minds are their wealth, not their body. They know and understand that their ideas and knowledge are the secret to success, not their physical attributes and qualities.

DISPENSATION OF VOICE OF VALUE

This Age of Information gives everyone an equal chance and opportunity for success, to decide the outcome of your life and destiny, to become influential and great, to chart your own course and create the life and future you desire. Never, in any dispensation, have men and women been in charge of their lives and destinies, and individually responsible and accountable for the outcome of their lives, than in this era. That is why it's an offence and crime against your mind to think that someone else is responsible for your destiny, or to blame another for the conditions of your life. You have exclusive power and prerogative to change the circumstances and conditions of your life, to decide who and what you will become, to imagine, design and ultimately construct the life you desire to lead. It's a dispensation of freedom of becoming who you want to become and achieve the dreams and desires in your mind.

Value is an intrinsic or internal thing; it comes from within, not without. It is the amount and quality of value you are able to add to yourself, and enhance the value of the lives of other people and improve the world around you, that determines the level of your success in life. Being able to reach a greater number of people and enlarge your coast of influence is what increases your worth and value to your world, not your colour and race. Value has nothing to do with your geographical location, religion, race or gender, but what you can mine out of your super-rich human mind. The reason your voice hasn't been heard yet is probably because you have not offered the world a value that can't be rejected. When people have need and problems, they don't care who has the solution before they pay for it, even if the person who can solve the problem is in a remote village somewhere. It doesn't matter any more. They would be found because value has a strong voice that can't be silenced and refuted, especially when it is critical.

Value is a universal language and currency that everyone understands and accepts English and French are not the real international languages, but 'value', because when you carry a value that people need, they will accept you and pay for it; they will understand you and respect you for it. If an employer has a problem in his organisation that is capable of ruining the business, or if they identify a skill or knowledge that will put them above their competitions and make them the leader in the market, even if the person that has that skill or knowledge has no formal education at all and living in the most remote village in any part of the world, they will find the person and pay for the whole expenses of bringing the person to occupy that position! His or her inability to speak English? Again, it doesn't count, as long as the person can deliver the value needed! What about a person's colour or race? Oh, sorry, it has become irrelevant! What if the employer had his family members or country men applying for that position? Sorry, he will ignore them because of the triumph of ideas and knowledge that this dispensation has brought us into. So, no one is your problem any more; you are now either your own enemy or friend, asset or liability.

> *Value is a universal language and currency that everyone understands and accepts*

It's because of this age that you can have a rich black skin and also a poor white skin; it's because of this age you can see a black person in higher positions of influence and authority over the white skin; it's because of this age that there is gender equality, where a woman can also do what a man can do. This age has brought to light the 'triumph of the qualified' and created room for equal opportunities for everyone, thereby making the most qualified the most suitable for any position. In the previous dispensations, the voices of the black race were not heard, but this age has changed that completely and amplified the voices of all races, so that the world can hear the voice of your ideas and knowledge, no matter where you are. It's a dispensation of 'voice of value' and 'voice of ideas and knowledge'. Anyone with value-adding ideas, knowledge and information can be heard, regardless of their age, gender, colour and race. So, to keep thinking that someone is responsible for your ugly situation is a mental sacrilege and trespass, for no one is responsible for your situation.

LEAVING YOUR FOOTPRINTS
'You may not be able to rewrite your history, but you can rewrite the future.'

It's the blessedness of this age that can make people who have been in subjugation, bondage, captivity, slavery, subservience and marginalisation to cry out for their freedom and protest against the injustices and cruelty done against them. It's because of this age that people who were once slaves can be their own masters; it's because of this age that those who were once poor can become rich and prosperous; those who were once slaves can become kings and queens; those who once ruled can also become rulers of themselves and others. It's because of this age that your voice can be heard from anywhere in the world, only if you have value-adding ideas and knowledge. It is because of this age that we can have super-billionaire black men and women in businesses, politics, media, and other aspects of human endeavours that were not possible in the past.

AFRICA, WE MUST BELIEVE IN OURSELVES TO RISE

All over the whole, we see and hear stories of black people making an outstanding impact and causing transformation in different areas of endeavours, and it's because of this dispensation of the triumph of ideas and knowledge we are in. It's because of this dispensation of the wealth of the mind that we see a lot of black people making their marks in their respective chosen careers, such as President Barack Hussein Obama, the 44th and first African American President of the United States; Britain's first black billionaire, Strive Masiyiwa; the American media mogul, Oprah Winfrey, known as the 'Queen of All Media', the richest African American of the 20th century and North America's first black multibillionaire; Lewis Hamilton, the most influential black person in the UK; Dr. Ngozi Okonjo-Iweala, the first woman and the first African to become the Director-General of World Trade Organization; Noah Harris, 21, first ever black man to be the student Body President at Harvard; the Nigerian billionaire businesswoman, Folorunsho Alakija; Vice President Kamala Harris, first black and woman Vice President of the United States; Afua Hirsch, a journalist and broadcaster in the UK, who uses her platform to write and speak on important issues in the black community; Richard Iferenta, Vice-Chairman of KPMG, a massive accounting organisation; Marcus Rashford, the Manchester United and England star footballer, who is campaigning for free school meals for children and also promoting reading by launching a children's book club; Dr. Kizzmekia S. Corbett, lead scientist on the modern Covid-19 vaccine team; Rosalind Brewer, Walgreen's next CEO and only black woman to currently lead a Fortune 500 firm, and lots of many other black people who are making their marks in different parts of the world.

The chances were very slim in the medieval age and past centuries. I wish to let the African race understand that they cannot continue to blame their colonial masters for their poverty and underdevelopment; to keep blaming someone or people for your undesirable conditions, after so many decades of your independence of them, is a crime against your rich, super-powerful mind. Your mind is richer than a goldmine; mine the riches of your mind and you will discover that you are richer than the owner of biggest goldmine or oil mine in any part of this world. It's a dispensation of the superiority of the mind, where the mind is your greater asset and has capacity for success. Therefore, since everyone is in charge of their minds and what they think and do, we are all responsible for what we become in life.

You have to decide that your own voice must be heard, and in which area of human endeavour you wish to make your mark. Don't believe anything can stop you; don't believe anyone is responsible for the situation of your life if you really want to change anything. The first step to changing your condition and circumstance of your life is by believing that it's within your power to do it, and you are responsible for the outcomes of your human existence.

YOUR MIND IS YOUR OWN 'GOLDMINE'

'I am a feminist, and what that means to me is much the same as the meaning of the fact that I am Black; it means that I must undertake to love myself and to respect myself as though my very life depends upon self-love and self-respect.'

June Jordan

We all have the same minds. The value of the human mind is the same because God created man equal. The human mind is the same for every one, but what we create out of the mind is what makes us different. Imagine if we have one million dollars to trade – the value of that money is the same, but our fate and future will depend on what we trade with the money, how we invest it, where we invest it, and how we manage it. That is the same with the human mind; it's the same value for everyone, whether black or white, but the difference depends

AFRICA, WE MUST BELIEVE IN OURSELVES TO RISE

on how we handle it, how we trade with it and manage it.

Some people use their minds to invent an aeroplane, an automobile, a television, a telephone and all the different inventions and gadgets we see today, while others use their own minds to beg others because they feel that is how they can meet their needs; yet, some others use their minds to invent evil things such as kidnapping, internet frauds, and other valueless things. Everything we see today is a product of someone's mind. Development is a product of someone's mind and imagination; and, in the same manner, poverty and underdevelopment are also products of people's minds.

So, the question is, what are you producing and doing with your mind? What are you creating and inventing with your mind? Here are you investing it and how are you managing your mind? These are what will determine your worth and value in life. Five years after President Goodluck Ebele Jonathan of Nigeria handed over to the present APC-led government under President Muhammadu Buhari, it's a disappointment that they still blame the previous administration for the present mess they have brought the country into. It's an abuse of the power of the human mind that they still accuse and blame the previous administration for the quagmire they have thrown the country into; and it's a greater disappointment and abuse of the superhuman mind of some of the leaders of Nigeria, and some African countries, to still blame their colonial masters for the precarious predicament they have plunged their nations into after many decades of independence.

> *Development is a product of someone's mind and imagination; and, in the same manner, poverty and underdevelopment are also products of people's minds.*

Someone might be responsible for the problem you might find yourself in, but they are not responsible for how you decide to respond to it; and it's not the problem that was created by others that matters, but how you respond to the problem.

Your approach towards the problem is what is crucial. Most times, the problems created by others may not be serious, but your approach and reactions toward it aggravate and worsen it. It's your response or reaction to a problem that will determine the weight and impact of the consequences. I agree that the colonial masters might have created the problem for their colonies, or be part of the cause of the problems that some of the African countries are facing, but I don't believe they should still be blamed after 60 years of independence, or even after twenty to thirty years of independence. Within these years, you created your own policies and made your own laws and executed them by yourselves, so why are you still holding others accountable for your actions?

'There is nothing like returning to a place that remains unchanged to find the ways in which you yourself have altered.'

Nelson Mandela

In a court of law, you can't accuse another person of influencing you and making you commit a crime for which you are being prosecuted. The jury does not acquit the person who committed a crime simply because he or she was advised or influenced by another person; no, they face the consequences of their actions. Likewise, it's time for Nigeria and the rest of the African race to own up to their mistakes and wrong decisions and policies, and accept their responsibilities for the growth and development of their states. It's time to stop the blame game, accusing and blaming their colonial masters for the injustices they think they had done to them. If someone advises you to do something wrong, it's your exclusive decision to decide either to do it or not, and whatever decision you make, you must be ready to accept the outcome and take responsibility for the consequences thereafter.

It is time to end the blame game. Nigeria can't continue

to blame the colonial masters for the mess they are in. There are elites in Nigeria, including Nobel Laureates and many other learned people. Nigeria has many world-renowned figures, like Dr. Ngozi Okonjo-Iweala, who is making global decisions that affect the whole world at the World Trade Organization; Nobel Laureate Prof. Wole Soyinka; Prof. Pat Utomi; and so many more intellectuals and elites. Nigeria has all it takes to transform herself from a third-word country to a first-world nation, just like Lee Kuan Yew did for Singapore, However, if we can't live together, then we can split if that is the solution, but we can't continue to blame other people for our mess.

CONCLUSION

You can't succeed in anything without self-belief and confidence, whether as an individual, group, organisation, or as a nation. The concept of self-belief is the foundation and secret of outstanding accomplishments and fulfilment in life. No one ever became great in life without first believing in themselves; it's the anchor of life and destiny. Without self-belief, you can never maximise your potentials and become the best you can be, for it takes confidence and belief in yourself to pursue your dreams and eventually fulfil your destiny. Self-belief is the secret of all personal achievements and accomplishments in life; it is the force of self-belief that will keep you going and striving for progress and success, even when no one can support and stand by you because they don't believe you can succeed. For instance, it took self-belief and confidence for Barack Obama, a black man, to become the first black president of the United States. According to him, in a zoom meeting 'Marcus Rashford meets Barack Obama' via Penguin Books, no one was born to be a president or something, we only grow to find ourselves and decide what we want to be in life, and it takes enough self-belief and confidence to do that or achieve anything great and extraordinary.

There will always be times when people will doubt you and your capacity to succeed, and it's normal for them to do so. There are times when people might not give you an opportunity or stake their chance on you, because they don't want to lose what they have; they don't believe you are worth the investment, support and benefit of the doubt. And that is when only your self-belief will take you through. There will be times when you will be doubted and left alone; in such times and seasons of isolation, only your self-belief and confidence will triumph.

CONCLUSION

The world likes to see proof. The world doesn't celebrate and recognise people when they are still passing through the process. You will only be acknowledged and rewarded in life when your process has brought you success, and only your belief in yourself can give you the patience, perseverance and persistence needed to pass through the process of life transformation. Passing through the process takes time and perseverance and, without first believing in yourself, your potentials, dreams and ideas, you will give up when the process becomes tough, or when you meet with temporary defeats and failures, and you will often meet them. Failures and defeats are integral and indispensable ingredients of success. Difficulties and challenges are inevitable on the path and process of success and fulfilment in life, and only your confidence in yourself and self-belief will provide the stamina and succour needed to pass through this stage of life.

It doesn't matter what you have passed through – don't give up. Rise up and take up your journey and get back onto the track of life and destiny, your generation is waiting to hear your voice. At the other end of your hardship and struggles is success, victory, prosperity, greatness and abundance, but you can't get there without passing through the road of criticism, rejection, isolation, difficulties, defeats and temporary failures. Whenever you fail, it's a sign that you are making progress and are a few steps closer to your success. Whenever you meet failure, remember you are a few feet away from gold. Gold is found deep within, so you have to dig deeper until you hit the flow.

The most important and crucial asset in fulfilling your destiny is believing in yourself, that you have all it takes to achieve it, that you can actually achieve anything you desire in life and become the best you can be. Having an unshakable, unyielding and unbreakable confidence and belief in yourself and in what you can do is the gateway to your world of unlimited possibilities and fulfilment of your life and destiny. Therefore, build your self-confidence, esteem and self-belief and never allow anyone to steal it away from you, because it's the destiny-capital that you will need, more than anything else, to achieve your dreams and fulfil your destiny.

ABOUT THE AUTHOR

Tim C. Oparaji is a Speaker, Author, Certified Trainer and Management and Leadership Consultant. He is a lifelong student and teacher of Leadership and Purpose, he developed the "TOPS MODEL" that explains the reason behind or cause of 'All Human Success and Failure' and "NEXT IDENTITY MODEL", a simple practical model that teaches people how to develop and transform their lives and become the best they can be.

He is called with the vision of Developing and Raising Leaders across the African continent and around the world by teaching people how to discover their purpose in life and develop their leadership potentials to fulfill it for an impactful living.

He is a member of Future Leaders Connect and Young African Leaders Initiative (YALI). He holds a Bachelor's degree in Project Management and he lives in the United Kingdom where he is currently studying for his master's degree in Healthcare Management at Swansea University.

Printed in Great Britain
by Amazon